Jewish Cooking from Here & Far

Traditions & Memories
from Our Mothers' Kitchens

**Congregation Beth Israel
Carmel, California**

By Congregation Beth Israel
Additional copies may be obtained at the cost of $13.95, plus
$3.00 postage and handling, each book. California residents add
$1.01 sales tax, each book.
Send to:
Congregation Beth Israel
5716 Carmel Valley Road
Carmel, CA 93923

Printed in the USA by

WIMMER
The Wimmer Companies, Inc.
Memphis • Dallas

Introduction

Once upon a time, a young man named Moishele, left his home and family in the old country, and started a search for his fortune in the form of diamonds. His journey was unsuccessful, and decades later, he returned home. His parents had passed away, his fiancee had married another, and was now a grandmother. He was grievously saddened by the failure of his life's mission.

His abandoned home was still standing, and so, sadly, he lay down to sleep the sleep of the weary and disillusioned. When he awoke, he went outside, as was his habit, to dig for diamonds, just as he had done each morning of his sad and lonely life in all the countries of the world that he had searched. And lo and behold — there they were, in his own back yard!

This home is the mythic home of the Jew. Some do not appreciate it while still in it, and venture far and wide to find diamonds of many sorts; on returning, they discover all the nourishment and riches necessary for life. Jews have lived the world over, in varied circumstances — often in extreme adversity and poverty —but the home was always a place of sustenance and enrichment and the sharing of love and family.

The latter has been the means through which traditional Jewish celebrations have survived and flourished — and most of these festivities and rituals that enhance and unify the family are centered around the kitchen. In this spirit and aware of the treasures that our traditional foods offer, we, at Congregation Beth Israel present the third of our cookbooks. The first was compiled in the sixties, the second *So Come to the Table* in the eighties, and now we have pleasure in publishing this volume:

Jewish Cooking from Here and Far:

Traditions and Memories from Our Mothers' Kitchens

The recipes in this book may not have been laboratory tested, but their merit has been established by the most critical groups of all — our families. We have gathered many new recipes from our members and have included a few of our favorites from the previous cookbooks. They reflect not only our past, but an awareness today of health issues that were not considered in times past, when people were only concerned about having enough food for survival and being able to stretch their meager portions to feed large families. In compiling a cookbook such as this, we could start by asking the question, what is Jewish cooking? Trying to answer this question, is nearly as daunting a task as trying to answer the question, what is a Jew? A trite answer is that Jewish food is whatever Jews eat and Jewish cooking is however they prepare it.

Just as Judaism has always been influenced by the places and times in which Jews find themselves, so too, the food we eat and the way we prepare it, carries remembrances of the places our ancestors have been. These places are far and varied. We are aware of the presence of our ancestors in Europe, both North and South, the Middle East, Australia and South Africa over the last centuries, but we now know of Jews in India dating back before the Common Era, and have records of a distinguished Jewish community in Kai Feng, China from the time of the Sung dynasty in 979. For Jews, in all times and places, the preparation and sharing of food has been and continues to be, a very important part of our family life. This is reflected in our teachings:

"You should eat and be full and you shall bless...."

As we wish to teach our children of the privilege of having food and making mealtimes sacred, traditionally we sing or recite the blessing, HaMotsi, over bread before each meal and over the special braided challah for the Shabbat. An important part of the Shabbat and festivals meal too, is wine over which we chant our thanks for the fruit of the vine. Each meal is concluded with the Birkat HaMazon — a prayer of thanksgiving for the meal just ended.

In this country, Jewish cooking can be described as "a melting pot," with a strong flavor of Eastern Europe, as the majority of Jews in this country are of Ashkenazic origin (Eastern European) rather than of Sephardic (Mediterranean) background. Hence, Americans generally associate bagels and lox, chicken soup and matzo balls, herring and cheese cake as Jewish food. However, these dishes represent but a small sampling of a very rich and varied tradition of food preparation. Jews from a Sephardic background may never have eaten gefilte fish, latkes or herring and would be equally surprised to know that many other Jews have never eaten couscous, borekas and mishmishiya.

Just as Jews have always learned to speak the language of the country in which they lived, they learned the regional styles of cooking, adapting as necessary to religious dietary laws of kashrut that call for the separation of milk and meat, the removal of blood from meat, and the exclusion of shellfish, game birds and pork.

Universally, chicken soup seems to be considered as a panacea, and no doubt dates back to the wonder of that warm, golden broth that would grace the Shabbat table in the shtetl. Another Shabbat favorite is cholent — a slow-cooking casserole dish that cooks overnight on Friday to be eaten hot on Saturday, without having to cook on Shabbat. In the cold of an Eastern European winter, a hot meal on Shabbat was essential. The usual cholent would be made of a little meat and a lot of vegetables. It is interesting to note that in the Yucatan such a dish is prepared on Friday for Saturday, although Judaism is not practiced by the people. A braided bread is also found there!

Jewish food was influenced by the difficult financial circumstances of shtetl life. In fact, from the Middle Ages onward, the majority of Jews lived in ghettoed Europe as the underprivileged poor. Jewish women's ingenuity created varied dishes with the little that was available and necessitated the development of many dishes that featured stuffed vegetables and soups that would help the little to go a long way. We have thus inherited a variety of recipes for chopped meats or fish. It is interesting to note that during the middle ages, Jews were strictly forbidden to buy fish as it was thought to increase fertility in Jewish males! During the week, shtetl Jews made do with a hunk of unrefined bread and soup or potatoes. This dark bread was replaced on Shabbat with the special white, braided challah, made from white flour and glazed with egg yolk and sprinkled with sesame or poppy seeds, representing the manna in the wilderness.

Chicken, available in the shtetl, was a staple, used first for soup and then eaten as a main course. This was served, together with fruit and vegetables, fresh when available, or otherwise, preserved. Shabbat was the highlight of the week. The sight of the challot (white braided breads) sitting between the Shabbat candles and next to the Shabbat wine was an uplifting experience for the family, who would savor foods not possible for them on a daily basis. They worked all week to make Shabbat special.

It can be argued that Judaism has always survived by adapting to modernity. Life has changed drastically in this century and this country. The staff of life from the 'old country' in many ways has become the stuff of nostalgia, as our concern for good health overrides our 'hamishe' leanings towards our past.

However, it need not be an 'either-or' dilemma. Another alternative is to change our way of preparing the old favorites. With this

in mind, we have included some low-fat versions of traditional dishes. The cholesterol level of any traditional dish can be lowered by the use of vegetable oil instead of schmaltz, egg substitutes, non-fat sour cream or yogurt, and non-fat cheese, such as cottage cheese....so, non-fat cream cheese allows us to have our cheese cake and eat it too! We recommend you convert any traditional dish in this manner. These substitutes create great dishes that you will be proud to serve and will fool your guests into thinking they are eating the "real thing".

In addition to altering the cholesterol level of our cooking, we can take advantage of the fresh produce that surrounds us, particularly here in California. Cilantro now graces our seder plates as the karpas, and the abundant and varied assortment of vegetables have become very popular — for many, replacing meat in their diets. Others choose tofu. Meat and fish, when prepared, are often broiled, and exotic vegetables are eaten raw. Monterey residents may be interested to know that at one time, in Italian communities, only Jews ate fennel, artichokes and eggplant — today, staples of Italian and international cuisine. Garlic too, was a staple flavoring for Jewish communities.

It may well be that our grandmothers would not feel at home in our kitchens with their modern appliances and substitute ingredients, but we want them to know that we treasure their recipes from the past which link us to them and our history, and helps us to span time and build bridges to our future.

Their recipes are the visual delights, the smells and the tastes of past birthdays, Shabbat dinners and Pesach seders. We want our grandmothers to know that even though we may be too busy or too health-conscious to cook as they did, the saving of their recipes for rereading and savoring is very important to us and to future generations. We honor our own ethnic cooking, reminding us who we are, and from where we have come.

The robust cuisine of our European past may be too heavy for our climate and media-dominated stereotypes on a regular basis — thus is our inimitable way, we adapt. On special occasions, however, such as our annual Jewish Food Festival at Congregation Beth Israel, we enjoy savoring our traditions of the past — calories and all — and so in keeping with our faith, we end with the traditional injunction "Es, mine kind, es" liberally translated as "Eat, eat and be merry".

Cookbook Committee

Linda Kaiser
Adeline Kohn
Joyce Kurtz
Judy Reibel
JoAnne Rockower
Esther Stern

Acknowledgements

Typists:
Ty Havas
Beny Neta
Ginny Rosenberg
Cath Tendler

Proofreaders:
Adeline Kohn
Joyce Kurtz
Cath Tendler
Bonni Weinstein

Batik Cover Art:
Amos Amit

Food Festival Photographer:
Martha Casanave

Writers:
Joyce Kurtz
Heather Mendel
Karen Wiskoff

Table of Contents

Appetizers

Sabbath

The importance of the celebration of the Sabbath cannot be underestimated. The Jewish essayist, Ahad Ha-Am once said, "more than the Jewish people have kept the Sabbath, the Sabbath has kept the Jewish people."

Sabbath, the weekly celebration of God's gift to us, is celebrated both in communal worship and at the home through what might have been the one good meal of the week and the chance to relax, enjoy one's family and sing praises to God.

The family has been the means through which traditional Jewish celebrations have survived and flourished. And as the family has preserved those celebrations through the ages, today these observances can greatly enhance and unify the family.

The Sabbath is the most important of our holidays and is the only one mentioned in the ten commandments. This may be the reason for its importance as well as the opportunity for connecting to God every week in this special way.

Traditionally the weekly day of rest gives family members the time together away from ordinary activities of the week. That separation and togetherness has never been more needed than in these days of our fast paced life. During the week each member of the family is busy doing their own thing. The Sabbath day provides the time to be together...time to talk and worship.

It begins on Friday evening by lighting and blessing at least two candles, symbolizing their bringing light and consciousness into our life.

The wine is blessed reminding us of the sweetness of life, and challah, the egg rich braided bread, is reserved as a special treat for Shabbat. Poor families would have saved and scrimped all week long for the

Sabbath evening meal. Traditionally chicken was boiled to make a soup and then the meat became the main course. The uniquely Jewish cholent, a Jewish cassoulet, is an ancient dish going back to biblical times and is traditionally served on Saturday afternoon, a day when no cooking is permitted. The dish would be put into the oven before sundown on Friday evening and left to cook slowly overnight, served warm and tasty.

In the winter a warm meal was essential. In the days before households had individual stoves the dish would be brought to the community baker and returned for the Saturday meal. The main ingredients are potatoes, beans, onions, and a little meat. Now we recognize the energy and health value of small amounts of meat and the positive value of legumes.

Chopped Chicken Liver

1 pound livers
5 tablespoons rendered
   chicken fat (or as needed)

2 onions, chopped
4 hard-boiled eggs
salt and pepper, to taste

Drain livers. Heat 2 tablespoons of fat in pan and brown onions. Remove the onions, adding more fat, if necessary, and cook livers on a medium heat. Chop livers, onions and eggs together, adding more chicken fat to bind. Season with salt and pepper.

Lee Rosenthal

Vegetarian Chopped Liver

2 cans green beans
1 large onion

½ cup chopped walnuts
3 hard boiled eggs

Sauté onion until slightly brown. Chop all ingredients until the consistency of chopped liver. Add salt and pepper to taste.

Anna Shelkowsky

What is...

GEFILTE FISH, a stuffed fish, is a concept that may date back to the Middle Ages. In 18th century Eastern Europe, gefilte fish was often a forcemeat made from chopped freshwater fish and matzo crumbs that was stuffed into slices of carp. Or it could be a whole carp stuffed with its own chopped flesh and flavorings and baked or poached. Today it is usually prepared as plain chopped fish balls not encased in a skin. Eating fish at the Friday Sabbath meal has been traditional since the Talmudic Era.

Baked Gefilte Fish

4 pounds carp, or other fatty
   type fish
4 jumbo eggs
1¹/₂ cups parsley
scant cup grated carrots
4 onions, chopped finely
1 tablespoon salt

4 teaspoons white pepper
1 teaspoon black pepper
1 teaspoon cayenne pepper
¹/₄ teaspoon cinnamon
¹/₂ teaspoon nutmeg
4 teaspoons minced garlic
1¹/₂ cups matzo meal

Have fish ground at fish market or grind the fish yourself. Mix with all other ingredients adding matzo meal last. Refrigerate. Form oval patties and sear patties on both sides to caramelize onions. Place in a shallow pan that has been oiled. Bake until golden in 375 degree oven. Serve hot, warm or cold with red horseradish, rye bread and dill pickles.

Carol Gilbert

Gefilte Fish

3¹/₂ pounds trout
2¹/₂ pounds sea bass, ling cod,
    snapper
4 medium onions
3 eggs (large)
1¹/₄ cups cold water
fish heads and bones

2 to 3 teaspoons salt
1 to 2 teaspoons white pepper
3 whole carrots
2 medium onions
1 teaspoon sugar
1 teaspoon paprika

Whitefish and pike are not available on the Monterey Peninsula. I substitute them with white-fleshed ocean fish, using a combination of fish available at the time.

Fillet and skin fish. Fish markets will fillet the fish for you. Grind fish and 2 onions into a chopping bowl. A Cuisinart can be used for the initial grinding. Chop in eggs, one at a time, with a small amount of water. Add salt and pepper and continue chopping until mixture does not adhere to chopping knife. Add additional salt and pepper to taste.

Use at least an 8 quart kettle. Combine fish heads, bones, carrots, 2 onions, sliced, sugar and paprika. Cover with cold water and bring to a boil. Add more water to fill kettle ¹/₃ full. Wet hands and make oblong balls of fish mixture and drop into boiling water and cook for 30 minutes. Taste juice and add more seasoning, if necessary. Shake kettle once or twice during cooking. Add boiling water, if necessary, during cooking period. Remove fish balls from pot while hot and pour some strained juice over them while they are cooling.

Makes about 36 fish balls.

Susan Gorelick

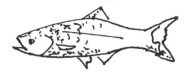

Quick Gefilte Fish

1 jar prepared gefilte fish   1 raw carrot
1 medium onion   pepper

Sauté onion in margarine until nicely browned. Cook sliced carrot. Add juice from jar of fish and pepper to taste. Simmer fish in mixture for 15 to 20 minutes. This should be made the day before serving.

When we were quite young we belonged to an Orthodox synagogue built in the late 1800s. The women were segregated from the men and sat in the balcony, which was a section with only four rows of benches that overhung the rear wall and extended half-way up each side of the synagogue. As a child, snuggled between my Mother and Grandmother, I felt safe and protected. The men below prayed with prayer shawls draped around their heads and bodies. They rocked slightly forwards and back as they prayed at their own pace. Occasionally the Rabbi would speak a line out loud so everyone could tell what part he was up to, and then off on their own again the men would continue.

On Saturdays when there was a Bar Mitzvah, the parents of the Bar Mitzvah boy would bring Hershey bars to hand out to all the children. We'd form a line and each child would be handed a candy bar. It was like getting gold!

Andrea Carter

Gefilte Fish

2 pounds pike
2 pounds whitefish
2 pounds winter carp or
    buffalo fish
1¼ teaspoons pepper
3 eggs

½ teaspoon sugar
2 teaspoons salt
¼ cup water
3 to 4 tablespoons matzo meal
1 to 2 finely chopped onions

Have fish mixture ground together. Add remaining ingredients. Put 2 quarts of water into a large pot. Add 5 onions, 2 teaspoons salt, ¼ teaspoon pepper, 4 carrots and include any fish bones including heads. With wet hands roll fish mixture into balls. Drop into fish stock. Cook loosely covered 1½ hours. Remove the cover and cook for 1½ hours more. Taste for seasonings.

Trudy Licht

Pescado Helado (Cold Fish)

½ cup chopped parsley
juice of 2 lemons
    (4 tablespoons)
1 (15-ounce) can tomato sauce
½ cup water
1 green pepper, chopped
    coarsely
¼ teaspoon pepper

2 teaspoons brown sugar,
    or to taste
3 cloves garlic, crushed
2 teaspoons vinegar, or to
    taste
2½ pounds fish filets
    (any kind)

In large pan combine all but fish, adjusting the sweet sour flavor, and boil 5 minutes. Add fish, lower heat and cook for 10 to 15 minutes until done. Carefully lift out fish and arrange in a decorative casserole dish. Boil down sauce until thickened and pour over fish. Chill overnight if possible and serve as a cold appetizer or for lunch with a cold rice salad.

Serves 8.

Ethel Alvy

Cold Sweet and Sour Salmon

1½ large onions
⅓ cup brown sugar
⅓ cup lemon juice
⅓ cup golden raisins
3 bay leaves
3 or 4 slices fresh ginger
2 teaspoons salt

6 to 8 cloves
3½ cups water, or as needed
1 cup fruity white wine
3½ to 4 pounds fresh salmon,
    either steaks or filets
2 lemons, cut in thin slices

Peel the onions and cut into thin slices and separate into rings. Combine with sugar, lemon juice, raisins, bay leaves, ginger, salt, cloves and water and simmer for 10 minutes, or until the onions are fairly soft. Add the fish and poach gently for 15 to 20 minutes, or until done but don't overcook. Remove the fish to a large glass baking dish so all pieces can lay in a single layer. Cover with lemon slices and pour the cooking liquid with all spices and onion over the fish. Chill overnight.

Serves 8 to 10 as a first course.

Recipe for a Happy Family

To equal quantities of generosity and thought for others, add a few dozen smiles, followed by the same number of kind words. Sprinkle freely with fun and merriment. Flavor with love and mix bright looks and serve to all.

Anna Shelkowsky

Sweet and Sour Fish

2 onions, thinly sliced
2 lemons, sliced
1/3 cup brown sugar
1/4 seedless white raisins
1 bay leaf
6 salmon steaks

2 teaspoons salt
2 cups water
6 gingersnaps, crushed
1/3 cup cider vinegar
1/4 cup sliced blanched
    almonds

Combine the onions, lemon slices, brown sugar, raisins, bay leaf, salmon steaks, salt and water in a saucepan. Cover and cook over low heat 25 minutes. Transfer to a large baking dish. Add the gingersnaps, vinegar and almonds to the fish stock. Cook over low heat stirring constantly, until smooth. Pour over the fish. Serve warm or cold.

Serves 6.

Linda Kaiser

Rojaldes (Filo Triangles)

1 pound filo
oil
1 beaten egg
grated Romano and/or
    Parmesan cheese
Potato Filling:
1 cup grated Romano and/or
    Parmesan cheese
2 to 3 pounds potatoes,
    cooked, drained and
    mashed

1/2 pound cottage cheese
1/2 teaspoon salt
2 eggs, beaten
Spinach Filling:
3 pounds spinach, cleaned,
    dried and chopped
1 pound cottage cheese or
    1/4 pound feta cheese
1 1/2 tablespoons flour
1 cup grated Romano and/or
    Parmesan cheese

Mix all filling ingredients together. If filo is frozen, allow to defrost in the refrigerator overnight, but fresh filo is easier to work with. Keep filo covered with a damp cloth while working. Place one sheet of filo on flat surface and dab lightly with oil. Place a second sheet evenly over the first, and with a sharp knife, cut filo into 6 equal strips. Place one heaping tablespoon of filling at lower corner of each strip. Fold filled corner into triangle. Continue folding triangle shapes to end of strip. Place rojaldes side by side in well-greased low-rimmed baking sheet. Brush tops with beaten egg, sprinkle with grated cheese. Bake in 350 degree oven for 20 to 25 minutes until golden brown and crispy. May be frozen.

Esther Stern

Mushroom Piroshke

8 ounces cream cheese
1/2 cup butter, at room
   temperature
1 1/2 cups flour
3 tablespoons butter
1 onion, finely chopped

1/2 pound mushrooms, finely
   chopped
1/4 teaspoon thyme
1/2 teaspoon salt
pepper, to taste
2 tablespoons flour
1/4 cup sweet or sour cream

Mix cream cheese and 1/2 cup butter until smooth. Add flour and work with fingers or pastry blender until smooth. Or process all ingredients at once in a food processor until dough forms a ball. Chill at least 30 minutes.

In sauté pan, heat remaining butter and lightly brown onions. Add mushrooms and cook about 3 minutes stirring often. Add thyme, salt and pepper and sprinkle with flour. Stir in cream and cook gently until thickened.

Preheat oven to 400 degrees. Roll out dough to 1/8 inch thickness on a floured cloth or board. Cut into 3 inch rounds. Place 1/2 to 1 teaspoon filling in the center and fold over in half and crimp edges with a fork. Piroshkes can be frozen at this point. Prick top crust to allow steam to escape. Place on ungreased baking sheet and bake until brown, about 15 minutes.

Diana Rosenthal

Sabbath Salmon Spread

6 1/2 ounces smoked salmon,
   flaked
1 (8 ounce) package cream
   cheese

1 1/2 teaspoons horseradish
1/3 onion, chopped fine

Blend first three ingredients together. Mix in onion. Cover and refrigerate overnight. Spread on warm bagels or challah.

Kerry Beren

Yalangis
(Stuffed Grape Leaves)

6 tablespoons canola oil
4 large onions, chopped
1 cup white rice
juice of 1 lemon
1 teaspoon salt

1/4 teaspoon pepper
3 cups water
1 jar grape leaves (8 ounces
   dry weight)

Using 4 tablespoons of the oil, sauté onions until golden. Add rice and half the lemon juice, salt, pepper, and 2 cups of water. Bring to a boil, cover, then simmer on low for 25 minutes. Let cool. Cut stems off leaves and lay on counter with veins up. Fill leaves with about 1 tablespoon of the filling, depending on the size of the leaves, which will vary. Fold into an envelope fold and place snugly seam down in large deep pot. (There will be several layers on top of each other). Combine remaining lemon juice, oil, and water. Pour over leaves. Weigh down with plate to fit within 1 inch of edge, to prevent floating. Bring to a boil, cover, then simmer for 30 minutes. Serve at room temperature as an appetizer.

Makes about 45 leaves.

Ethel Alvy

Hummus

2 1/2 cups canned chick peas,
   drained
3 tablespoons light sesame oil
   or olive oil
4 tablespoons lemon juice

2 cloves garlic, crushed
1/2 teaspoon salt
1 tablespoon chopped parsley
paprika

Put all ingredients in a blender and puree until smooth. Refrigerate for 8 hours before serving. Sprinkle with paprika and parsley.

Makes 4 servings.

Jeannine Ushana

Hummus-Chick Pea Tahini

1 (20 ounce) can cooked chick
  peas
2 tablespoons chick pea
  packing liquid
1/2 cup fresh lemon juice, or
  less to taste

2 cloves garlic, coarsely
  minced
3/4 teaspoon salt
1/2 cup sesame tahini
chopped parsley or paprika
  for garnish

Drain the chick peas but save the liquid. Puree the chick peas, 2 tablespoons packing liquid, lemon juice, garlic and salt. Add more packing liquid if necessary to facilitate blending. Add the sesame tahini and blend into the chick pea mixture. Serve with pita bread, crackers and raw vegetables

Linda Kaiser

Eggplant Tahini (Baba Ganoush)

1 medium eggplant (1 pound)
6 tablespoons tahini
6 tablespoons water
1 garlic clove crushed

3 tablespoons fresh lemon
  juice
1/2 teaspoon salt
2 tablespoons chopped parsley

Grill the eggplant over a gas flame or under broiler until the skin is black and blistery. The inside will be soft. Peel off the charred skin and scoop out the pulp. Squeeze the pulp to remove the bitter juices. Combine the eggplant pulp with the remaining ingredients except the parsley and blend well. Garnish with the chopped parsley and serve with sesame crackers, triangles of pita or cracker bread.

Mohamra

3 large cloves garlic
2 cups ground walnuts
3 medium red peppers, seeded
  and chopped coarsely
1 medium onion, chopped
  coarsely

1/2 to 1 small jalapeno,
  chopped
2 tablespoons molasses
2 tablespoons olive oil
1 tablespoon ground cumin
salt, to taste

Blend first five items in food processor until pureed. Transfer to a bowl and add the rest. Serve with pita. This keeps well in the freezer.

Kerry Beren

Red Pepper Spread

2 tablespoons olive oil
3 large onions
1 (7¼ ounce) jar roasted red
    peppers or 4 large red
    peppers roasted with 3
    tablespoons red wine
    vinegar added

2 tablespoons tomato paste
¼ teaspoon thyme
3 tablespoons lemon juice
black pepper
8 ounces cream cheese

Sauté onions in oil until limp and golden. Combine with all other ingredients in blender and serve with hearty grain bread.

Kerry Beren

Eggplant Dip

1½ pounds eggplant
2 teaspoons olive oil
½ onion, chopped
2 cloves garlic
1 red or green pepper, minced
3 tomatoes, chopped

2 tablespoons tomato paste
1 teaspoon honey
¼ cup balsamic vinegar
pepper, allspice, lemon juice
    and lemon zest to taste

Pierce the eggplants a few times and bake in a 450 degree oven for 20 to 30 minutes or until soft. Cool. Cut in half and scoop out the pulp and chop. Heat oil, sauté the onions, garlic, pepper and add remaining ingredients to the eggplant; adding pepper, allspice, lemon juice and zest to taste. Garnish with additional lemon zest, and peppers. Serve with pita or corn chips.

Joyce Kurtz

Eggplant Appetizer

1 large eggplant, pierced
2 tablespoons chopped onion

1 tablespoon extra virgin
    olive oil
salt to taste

Broil the eggplant, turning every 10 or 15 minutes until skin is lightly charred. Remove from broiler, cool and then peel. In a chopping bowl, place the peeled eggplant, onion, olive oil and salt and chop until smooth. Refrigerate. Serve with assorted crackers.

Adeline Kohn

Meat Balls

1 pound grape jelly
1 can chili sauce
2 pounds ground beef
1 cup water

garlic powder
mustard
salt

Put mustard, salt and garlic into ground beef and mix well. Use a little water or tomato juice if meat is too thick. Bring jelly, chili sauce and water to a boil and drop meat balls into mixture. Cook until meat is fluffy, check by cutting meat ball in half.

Trudy Licht

Sweet and Sour Meatballs

1 pound ground beef
1 envelope onion soup mix
1/2 cup matzo meal
1/2 cup water
1 egg
parsley, salt, pepper and
   garlic powder
2 onions, medium chopped

28 ounces canned tomatoes
16 ounces canned tomato
   sauce
2 tablespoons sugar
1/2 teaspoon sour salt
   (ascorbic acid)
1 bay leaf
1 clove garlic, crushed

Mix the first six ingredients and shape into balls. Sauté onions in oil. Add whole tomatoes, crushed, and tomato sauce. Slowly bring to boil. Add sugar and sour salt (add more to taste), bay leaf and garlic. Add meatballs to sauce and simmer until done.

Joyce Kurtz

Cayenne Pecans

pecans
powdered sugar
hot peanut oil

sea salt
cayenne pepper

Blanch pecans for about 3 minutes. Strain and coat in powdered sugar. Add to hot peanut oil (350 degrees); cook till golden brown. Drain and add sea salt and cayenne pepper to taste.

Kerry Beren

Caponata

1/3 cup extra virgin olive oil
3 to 4 cloves garlic, finely
   chopped
1 cup chopped onions
2 cups eggplant, finely
   chopped
1 medium zucchini, cubed
1 red pepper, roasted,
   skinned and chopped

4 cups fresh tomatoes, seeded,
   skinned and chopped
3 tablespoons currants
1 tablespoon sugar
2 tablespoons capers
1 tablespoon balsamic
   vinegar

Heat oil and add garlic and onions; sauté briefly. Add eggplant, zucchini and red peppers. Turn up heat and stir constantly long enough to sear all ingredients. Add tomatoes, currants, sugar and capers and cook over low heat 15 to 20 minutes. You may need to thin a little with water. Remove from heat and add vinegar. This is great with pita bread or tortilla chips for an appetizer. For a main course pasta sauce, add roasted chicken or sausage.

Fritatta à la Lorraine

1 bunch green onions, finely
   chopped
1/2 cup parsley, finely chopped
6 eggs, beaten
3/4 pounds sharp cheddar
   cheese

salt and pepper, to taste
dash of hot pepper sauce
6 soda crackers, crushed
2 jars artichoke hearts
   marinated in olive oil

Sauté onions and parsley in oil from the artichoke hearts. Blend all ingredients but artichoke hearts in blender for a few moments until thoroughly mixed. Cut up artichoke hearts and fold into mixture. Pour into a greased glass baking dish and bake in a 350 degree oven for about 40 minutes. Cut into one-inch squares and serve hot or cold. This can be frozen. Thaw first, then cover with foil and warm in medium oven for a few minutes.

Charles Blum

Goldie's Quick and Easy Chopped Herring

1 pound jar herring fillets in
  wine sauce
1/2 pint sour cream
2 sweet bermuda or Vidalia
  onions, sliced

1/2 cup white or cider vinegar
3 tablespoons sugar
2 hard boiled eggs, chopped

Combine all ingredients and refrigerate. You can use non-fat sour cream, artificial sweetener and 3 chopped hard boiled egg whites to make a wonderful version low in fat and cholesterol.

Bonni Weinstein

Gravlax

2 to 3 pounds salmon filets
1 bunch fresh dill, coarsely
  chopped
1 teaspoon dill seed
1 teaspoon dried dill weed

2 tablespoons kosher salt
1/4 teaspoon pepper
2 tablespoons sugar
1/4 teaspoon allspice
1/2 cup vodka

Mix salt, sugar, pepper, allspice together and sprinkle one half of the mixture on the bottom of a glass baking dish. Lay one half the chopped dill on top. Place the filets on the dill in a single layer if possible, skin side down, and top with remaining dill. Pour vodka over all and cover with plastic. Refrigerate four days turning once or twice a day. To serve: remove spices and slice at an angle as you would slice smoked salmon. This may be frozen to last longer, if you don't eat it first.

Charles Blum

Soups
& Salads

Rosh Hashanah

According to tradition, Rosh Hashanah is the anniversary of creation, or in other words the birthday of the human race. Jewish New Year provides us the opportunity to take stock of our relations with others and make changes and to begin to renew our spiritual selves. We begin the year among our family and close friends. According to tradition everything one does is written down in the Book of Life. On Rosh Hashanah those deeds are examined in Heaven. The good and bad deeds of the previous year are weighed and judged. "On Rosh Hashanah it is written and on Yom Kippur it is sealed...who shall live and who shall die...but repentance, prayer, and charity temper Judgement's severe decree." The traditional Rosh Hashanah greeting "May you be inscribed for a good year" has a particularly deep meaning.

Apples, traditionally a symbol of fertility, are dipped in honey, because in ancient times they were said to have had regenerative powers, and a challah in a round form, as a symbol of life without end, are traditionally served.

Yom Kippur

Yom Kippur is observed rather than celebrated. This Holy Day, the most solemn of the Jewish year, ends the ten day penitential period that begins with Rosh Hashanah. It is during these ten days that Jews reflect on their past years wrongs. It is said "forgiveness is not given until asked for from those you might have harmed." Synagogue prayers are in the plural, no one is exempt as the congregation prays for absolution for sins, committed "knowingly or unknowingly." It is considered the most important day of the calendar even by those who observe seldom or at no other time.

Traditionally, Yom Kippur is a day of fasting and no

cooking or eating is done. With the final sounding of the shofar, the ram's horn, the end of the day of prayer is announced, and the twenty four hour fast is customarily broken by eating something sweet, symbol of a sweet year to come.

What is...

BORSCHT's name comes from a Russian word meaning cow parsnips. For Russian, Lithuanian and Polish Jews, beetroots (borscht), cabbage (sauerkraut), and sorrel (schav) made up a category of foods known as sours. Their flavors counterbalanced the dull taste of the black bread and potatoes that were the mainstays of the daily diet.

Carrot Borscht

4 medium carrots, peeled and
   sliced
1 cup boiling water
½ teaspoon salt
2 tablespoons onion, finely
   chopped
1½ teaspoons chopped fresh
   mint (or ¾ teaspoon dry
   mint)

2 tablespoons melted butter
   or margarine
2 tablespoons flour
1 cup vegetable broth
1 cup milk
¼ teaspoon ground nutmeg
salt, to taste
¾ cup orange juice

Cook carrots in water and salt until tender. Whirl carrots and cooking liquid smooth in a blender. In a saucepan sauté onion and mint in butter until soft. Mix in flour and stir until bubbly; gradually adding vegetable broth and milk, the carrot mixture and nutmeg. Simmer over medium-low heat, stirring for 3 minutes. Add salt to taste and stir in orange juice. Serve with a dollop of sour cream or yogurt.

Serves 4.

Barbara Taylor

Beet Borscht

8 small beets
4 cups boiling water
salt, to taste

½ cup mild vinegar or ¼ cup
lemon juice or ¼ teaspoon
citric acid crystals
½ to 1 cup sugar, to taste

Cover beets with water and boil until tender. Remove beets from pot and strain liquid into soup pot. Slip beet skins off and grate beets on fine grater into the beet juice (which has been strained). Add 1 tablespoon salt and 4 cups boiling water. Bring to quick boil, reduce heat and cook 5 minutes. Add vinegar and sweeten to taste. Cool and chill in closed jars. Add 1 or 2 tablespoons sour cream and boiled potato to each plateful just before serving.

Lillian Ullman

Spinach Borscht

10 ounces frozen chopped
spinach
6 cups cold water
2 teaspoons salt,
or to taste
lemon juice, to taste

1 bunch green onions, finely
sliced (including white
portion)
8 ounces cucumber, peeled
and diced
8 ounces sour cream or plain
yogurt

Place the frozen spinach in a kettle with the water and salt and cook on low heat until the spinach is thawed. Separate the spinach, then turn up the heat and bring to a boil. Turn heat back to low and simmer about 7 minutes. Remove from the stove and cool completely. Add more salt if necessary, the sliced green onions, and lemon juice to taste. (This borscht will not taste "right" until it is cold, so there is a bit of guesswork in adding the lemon juice just after cooking. I use 3 tablespoons of lemon juice to start, because I like the tart lemon flavor. The taste can always be corrected after the borscht is chilled.) Refrigerate until ready to serve. Serve borscht well chilled mixed with diced cucumber and topped with a dollop of sour cream or plain yogurt.

Karen Wiskoff

Beef Borscht

3 pounds short ribs
2 or 3 large onions, chopped
salt and pepper
1 whole bunch celery
1 medium-sized cabbage,
    thinly sliced

5 or 6 cans whole beets
    (julienne)
sugar and sour salt
dill weed
4 or 5 boiling potatoes, cut in
    pieces

Sear short ribs with fat side down on high heat. Add oil, if necessary. Add onions to searing short ribs and season with salt and pepper. Add carrots, celery and cover with water. Cook until vegetables are soft and remove them. Add cabbage to soup as well as the beets and their juice. Cook slowly. Don't expect it to be too red, as the cabbage absorbs color. Add sugar and sour salt to taste (enough to make it sweet and sour). Add dill weed and more salt, if necessary. Add potatoes about one hour before the soup is to be served. Dill weed spinkled on top.

This soup should be cooked the day before you wish to serve it so you may skim off the fat from the meat.

Carol Gilbert

Sweet and Sour Cabbage Soup

2 pounds short ribs
2 medium onions, thinly
    sliced
1 medium head cabbage,
    thinly sliced or shredded
1 (28 ounce) can crushed
    tomatoes in puree

56 ounces (two empty tomato
    cans) water
4 cups brown sugar
1 cup reconstituted lemon
    juice
$1/2$ to 1 teaspoon salt (+ or - to
    taste)

Spray bottom of soup pot with non-stick cooking spray. Sear meat on both sides. Add onions and sauté lightly. Add remaining ingredients. Cover and bring to boil. Lower to simmer and cook two hours.

Serves 8 to 10.

Ronnie Ramistella

Cabbage Soup

1 head of cabbage, rinsed, cored and cut up

2 large onions, peeled and sliced

2 cans Italian tomatoes, peeled and cut, use all liquid

2 cans tomato soup

16 ounces water or soup stock

1 tablespoon caraway seeds

2 teaspoons cinnamon

juice of 1 or 2 lemons

sugar, 1 tablespoon to each lemon (sweet and sour to taste)

In a large pot, brown the onions well, add cabbage, cover and let it cook down a while. Add the rest of the ingredients and cook over low heat for at least 2 hours. Taste and mix every once in a while.

Adeline Kohn

This recipe comes from my father's side of the family. He was born in Bessarabia, Russia, at the time, close to the Romanian border. His three sisters in New York were all good cooks and they made this soup. They gave it to my mother who gave it to me. It can also be made with lean short ribs, browned with the onions, and fat can be skimmed when cool. My aunts never measured anything too carefully. Try it. It worked.

Adeline Kohn

Lentil Soup

1 cup chopped onion
2 carrots, chopped
8 ounces smoked turkey or
    chicken sausages
2 tablespoons oil
16 ounces chicken stock
3 cups water

1 cup applesauce
1¼ cups dried lentils
¼ cup sherry
1 teaspoon basil
½ teaspoon marjoram
salt and pepper, to taste

Cook onion, carrot and sausage in oil in large pan until vegetables are tender and sausage lightly browned. Add chicken broth, water, applesauce and lentils. Cover and simmer 30 minutes. Add sherry, marjoram and basil. Simmer 15 to 20 minutes until tender. Season with salt and pepper.

Makes 8 to 10 servings.

Joyce Kurtz

Chicken or Beef Barley Soup

2 pounds soup meat or 2 cut-
    up skinned chickens
3 to 4 soup bones
1 package barley soup mix
2 to 3 minced garlic cloves
2 small onions
4 carrots

2 celery stalks
2 tablespoons Worcestershire
    sauce
2 tablespoons parsley
⅔ cup barley
1 bay leaf
salt and pepper, to taste

Put meat and bones in a large kettle. Salt well. Add 4 quarts water. Bring to a boil. Skim. Simmer 1½ hours. Add vegetables and simmer 1 hour more. Remove vegetables, puree and return to broth. Cut the meat up and return to broth. Add soup mix, barley and seasonings and simmer 1 hour more. Remove bay leaf and adjust seasonings.

Linda Kaiser

Rosenthal Chicken Soup

1 pound chicken carcasses,
   preferably breasts
1 large onion
3 stalks celery
2 carrots

1 to 2 parsnips
1 clove garlic
4 to 5 peppercorns
salt, to taste

Place washed chicken in large pot and cover with water. Bring to a fast boil and skim off the scum that rises to the top. Rough chop onion, celery, carrots, and parsnips and add to soup with garlic and peppercorns and 1 teaspoon salt (optional). Simmer for 2 to 3 hours and keep water level just covering ingredients. Strain soup through a sieve and chill to congeal fat on top. Before serving remove fat and save for matzo balls.

Serves 6.

Diana and Rick Rosenthal

Russian Mushroom-Barley Soup

3 quarts water
1½ pounds stew meat, cubed
2 medium onions, quartered
3 carrots, scrubbed

5 stalks celery
1½ cups mushrooms, sliced or
   ¾ cup dried mushrooms
1½ cups pearl barley

Boil the stew meat in salted water (some knuckle bones or the marrow-filled soup bones make a nice addition), skim the fat. Slice the carrots and celery into large, chunky pieces, and add to the boiling stock. Add the onions, mushrooms and barley. Season to taste with salt and pepper and simmer over low heat. If too thick, when barley has finished absorbing liquid, add more water. Serve with rye bread.

It's even better the next day, for reasons known only to the Divine One and the Russian Jews!)

A stick-to-the-ribs budget meal-in a-dish for the winter months. Our European ancestors would harvest forest mushrooms in the autumn and dry them for use throughout the winter. Dried mushrooms have a more pungent flavor, but fresh are quite adequate.

Rabbi Mark Gross

During the war we lived with my Bobu, my mother's mother, and she and I developed a very special bond. Judaism was her whole life and everything she did revolved around religion. I have many wonderful memories, but the one I relish the most deals with Yom Kippur and schlaging kaporos. I can still see my mother, my Bobu and myself sitting in the kitchen with Bobu swinging a dead chicken over our heads saying some prayer in Hebrew. She would swing the chicken three times in the theory that all our sins would go to the chicken. The one question that always resonated in my head was wouldn't we get the sins back when we ate the chicken? However, being a shy child I never asked and dutifully ate the chicken. After all it was a 'sin' not to eat all the food when there were children starving in other parts of the world.

After several years of swinging the chicken, we became modern and my Bobu would wrap coins in a hanky and we would swing that around our heads and then I would have the honor of putting the coins in the pushkes, that she had tacked up on the banister leading to the basement. Several times a year an old Jewish man would come and collect the money and give it to the poor. I liked this approach much better as I could now eat my chicken with no feelings of guilt and feel proud of helping others.

Natalie Lehrner Jaffe

Cool Cucumber Soup

2 medium cucumbers,
   unpeeled and diced
2 or 3 green onions, sliced
   (include tops)
1 small clove garlic, minced
   or crushed

1 to 2 sprigs of mint,
   if available
1 cup half and half
juice of 1 lemon
2 cups plain yogurt

Place cucumbers, onions, garlic and mint in blender. Whirl until no large pieces remain. Pour in half and half and whirl an additional minute. Stir in lemon juice and yogurt. Serve chilled and garnish with additional mint sprigs.

Serves 3 to 4.

Barbara Taylor

My son, the banker, whose arm must be broken because he never writes to his mother, made this soup in his college days when everything he ate depended upon his blender, a hot plate and an apartment-size refrigerator that worked best if it contained a block of ice like one the iceman delivered to Gramma's kitchen. Except where do you find an iceman these days? So instead, he went to a supermarket where he could buy cold ingredients and meet pretty girls and ask them if they knew how to make cucumber soup. Why cucumber soup? Because his friend, Mark, was into gardening and was always giving away cucumbers.

Barbara Taylor

Toasted Golden Squash Soup

about 2½ pounds yellow
fleshed winter squash,
such as butternut or acorn
squash
2 tablespoons olive oil
2 medium (about 1 pound)
Pippin or other tart
apples, unpeeled and cut
in half

2 small (about ¾ pounds)
onions, unpeeled and cut
in half
½ cup hazelnuts
3 cups regular strength
chicken broth
1 cup apple juice

Cut squash in half lengthwise, if shell is hard, tap the blunt edge of knife with mallet to drive it through. Scoop out and discard seeds and strings. Heat oil in 10x15 inch rimmed pan in a 400 degree oven. Lay squash skin side down, put apple and onion halves beside squash. Bake until squash is very tender when pierced about 1½ hours.

Bake hazelnuts for about 10 minutes until browned and set aside. Let squash stand until cool enough to touch and scoop flesh from shell. Scrape apple from skins and pull off onion skins; discard shell and skins. Put all through food processor. Add enough broth to help make a very smooth puree.

Pour puree, remaining broth, and juice into a saucepan. Stir over medium high heat until steaming. Ladle into bowls and sprinkle with nuts.

Makes 6 servings.

Joyce Kurtz

Augolemono Soup

6 cups chicken broth
½ cup rice
salt, to taste

2 eggs
juice of 1 lemon

Bring broth to boil and add rice. Simmer until rice is tender. Add salt to taste. Beat eggs well. Add lemon juice to eggs and beat thoroughly. Dilute with a little stock, beating constantly with a wire whisk or fork. Add a little more soup, beating well. Add to remainder of soup, stirring constantly. Reheat soup but **do not boil**.

Esther Stern

Bell Pepper Soup

3 red bell peppers
2 cups chopped leeks
1 tablespoon butter
2 teaspoons oil
1 cup vegetable stock

3 cups buttermilk
2 teaspoons soy sauce
fresh ground white pepper
fresh dill
1 sliced lime

Simmer bell peppers and leeks in oil, covered, for 15 minutes. Add butter and broth and simmer for 30 minutes, keeping it partially covered. Put the mixture in a blender or food processor and blend. Allow to cool and strain. Chill. Add buttermilk, soy sauce and ground pepper. Serve topped with a slice of lime and sprinkled with fresh dill.

Serves 6.

JoAnne Rockower

Tomato Bouillon

½ cup thinly sliced onions
2 tablespoons butter
1 (1 pound, 12 ounce) can
  Italian style tomatoes
1 (10½ ounce) can condensed
  beef broth

1 cup water
½ teaspoon salt
¼ teaspoon dried dill
⅛ teaspoon white pepper
grated Parmesan cheese

Sauté onions in butter slowly until soft but not brown. Drain liquid from tomatoes into onions. Add broth, water, salt, dill and pepper. Heat to boiling. Chop tomatoes and add to soup. Cover and simmer on low heat for 10 minutes. Serve hot with sprinkling of Parmesan in each bowl.

Cathleen Connell

Cream of Smoked Salmon Soup

1 can cream of mushroom
  soup
1 can tomato bisque
2 soup cans milk, half and
  half or cream

less than ¼ cup vermouth
  (optional)
¼ teaspoon dill weed
chopped chives
smoked salmon

Mix soups and liquids together and begin to heat. Chop smoked salmon. The amount you use depends on how rich you feel at the moment, but ¼ pound is more than enough. Add dill and heat well through. Top with chives and enjoy.

Joyce Kurtz

No-Fat Oriental Dressing

5 ounces rice wine vinegar
2 ounces soy sauce
¼ teaspoon ginger
1 package sweetener

dash thyme
1 tablespoon chopped
  cilantro

Mix the soy sauce with the rice wine vinegar, spices and cilantro. Pour over salad greens.

JoAnne Rockower

Eggplant Salad

1 large eggplant
1 small onion, chopped
1/4 cup olive oil

3 tablespoons wine vinegar
chopped parsley
salt and pepper, to taste

Bake a large eggplant in a preheated 350 degree oven 1 hour or until soft. Pierce the eggplant several times to allow the steam to escape. Dip it into cold water and peel off the skin. Add 1 small chopped onion, 1/4 cup olive oil and 3 tablespoons wine vinegar and salt and pepper to taste. Mix well. Mound on a platter and sprinkle with chopped parsley. Surround with tomato wedges and black olives. You can also sprinkle with feta cheese and serve with crisped pita.

Linda Kaiser

Eggplant Salad

2 pounds eggplant
1 tomato
1 green bell pepper
2 scallions, chopped
1 teaspoon salt

1/4 teaspoon pepper
1/4 cup lemon juice
1/4 cup parsley, snipped
1 teaspoon garlic powder

Rinse eggplants and pat dry. Roast on foil in oven at 400 degrees. Turn occasionally so that eggplant will be tender on all sides. Roasting time is around 40 minutes. Scoop out the flesh and immediately pour lemon juice over it to prevent discoloring. Mash the flesh with a wooden spoon and let cool. Before serving, add all the vegetables (chopped) and the seasonings. Serve plain or with pita bread.

Carol Gross

Tabbouleh (Cracked Wheat Salad)

1 cup cracked bulgur wheat
Dressing:
³/₄ cup olive oil or salad oil
3 tablespoons lemon juice
1 clove garlic, crushed
1¹/₂ teaspoons salt
¹/₂ teaspoon pepper
³/₄ cup scallions, finely
  chopped

1 cup cucumbers, pared and
  cut into ¹/₄ inch cubes
1¹/₂ cups parsley, finely
  chopped
³/₄ cup fresh mint, finely
  chopped
4 tomatoes, medium, peeled
  and cut into ¹/₂ inch cubes
fresh mint sprigs

Rinse bulgur under cold water; drain well. Turn into a large bowl. Cover with boiling water. Let bulgur soak 1 to 2 hours. Drain; squeeze out excess moisture with your hands.

Dressing: In a medium bowl, combine olive oil, lemon juice, garlic, salt and pepper. Mix well.

Add bulgur to dressing. Toss lightly to mix well. Turn into a large glass bowl. Mix all ingredients and refrigerate, tightly covered, overnight. Serve with lettuce.

Serves 10 to 12.

Jeannine Ushana

Black Bean, Corn and Pepper Salad

2 (15 ounce) cans black beans
  or white kidney beans,
  drained and rinsed
1¹/₂ cups corn kernels
1 large red bell pepper,
  stemmed, seeded and diced
2 small fresh jalapeño peppers,
  stemmed, seeded and
  minced

³/₄ firmly packed chopped
  cilantro
¹/₄ cup lime juice, or more to
  taste
2 tablespoons salad oil
salt and pepper and garlic,
  minced

Mix in a bowl the beans, corn, red pepper, jalapeño, cilantro, lime juice, oil and salt and pepper. Add garlic. Use extra lime juice or a little rice vinegar and a little sugar. Taste and adjust seasonings. Chill, covered for at least an hour or overnight. Serve on platter or in bowl lined with lettuce leaves and ground black pepper as a garnish.

Kerry Beren

Russian-Style Potato and Artichoke Salad

10 small new potatoes,
  roasted
1 cup green peas, blanched
8 freshly cooked artichoke
  hearts, quartered or
  1 (14 ounce) can artichoke
  hearts, drained and
  quartered

½ cup plain yogurt
¼ cup low-fat mayonnaise
¼ cup non-fat sour cream
2 tablespoons chopped fresh
  dill or 1 teaspoon dillweed
salt and coarsely ground
  black pepper

Rub oil on potatoes and roast at 400 degrees on baking pan 45 minutes to 1 hour. (Test for doneness with fork.)

When cool enough to handle, arrange half of the potatoes, peas and artichoke hearts on a platter. Combine remaining veggies in large bowl. In a small bowl, blend yogurt, mayonnaise, sour cream and dill. Season with salt and pepper to taste. Toss veggies in bowl with dressing, then place next to the undressed veggies. Chill until serving time.

Serves 6 to 8.

Barbara Taylor

Curried Rice Salad

1 tablespoon olive oil
1 teaspoon curry powder
13¼ ounces chicken broth
1 cup chopped celery
1 cup raw white rice

½ cup water
½ cup toasted slivered
  almonds
⅔ cup raisins
⅓ cup mayonnaise

After heating the oil in a saucepan add curry and heat gently for 1 minute. Add broth, celery, rice and water. Heat to boil. Lower heat and simmer covered until liquid has been absorbed. Chill 6 hours or more. Stir in remaining ingredients.

Serves 6 to 8.

Top Ramen Cabbage Salad

1 package Top Ramen with
  seasonings
1/2 or less green cabbage,
  sliced thin
1/2 or less red cabbage, sliced
  thin
2 to 3 green onions, sliced
2 to 3 pieces celery, sliced

2 to 3 tablespoons sesame
  seeds
1 package sliced almonds
1/2 cup salad oil
2 tablespoons vinegar
2 tablespoons sugar
dash salt, pepper and garlic
  salt

Mix cabbage, onions and celery together in a large salad bowl. Crumble the noodles and add to the salad.

On a cookie sheet or in a toaster oven roast the sesame seeds and almonds until they are golden brown; add them to the salad mixture.

Mix together the oil, vinegar, sugar and spices and add the seasoning mix from the Top Ramen packet; pour over the cabbage and mix well.

JoAnne Rockower

Black-eyed Pea Salad

2 cups black-eyed peas,
  cooked and drained
2 cloves garlic, crushed
1 tablespoon chopped parsley

3 tablespoons oil
juice of 1 lemon
salt and pepper, to taste

Mix all ingredients together and serve cold.

Esther Stern

Green Salad Bowl

2 heads lettuce
1 bunch chicory
1 cucumber, peeled and sliced
1 green pepper
3 tomatoes
1 can drained anchovies
French Dressing:
1 cup vegetable oil (or 1/2 cup vegetable oil and 1/2 cup olive oil)

1/4 cup tarragon vinegar
1 teaspoon salt
1 teaspoon sugar
1 clove garlic, split
1 teaspoon paprika
1/2 teaspoon dry mustard
1 tablespoon grated onion
1 tablespoon Worcestershire sauce

Tear lettuce; cut chicory in small pieces and combine with cucumber. Place all ingredients in a bowl, toss lightly and arrange sliced green pepper rings and quartered tomatoes over salad. Garnish with strips of anchovies.

Dressing: Place all dressing ingredients in a jar and shake thoroughly. Remove garlic before serving. To serve, pour dressing over greens, toss until thoroughly mixed.

Serves 8.

Adeline Kohn

Turkish Salad

4 tomatoes, diced
1 red onion, diced
1 cucumber, diced
1 green pepper, diced

Dressing:
juice of 1 lemon
2 tablespoons olive oil
1 teaspoon salt
freshly ground pepper

Mix dressing ingredients and pour over vegetables 30 minutes before serving. Toss and serve cold.

Esther Stern

Coleslaw Jardiniere

3 cups cabbage, shredded
2 carrots, grated
1 green pepper, chopped
2 tablespoons onion, grated
2 tablespoons parsley, minced

Dressing:
1 cup mayonnaise
3 tablespoons tarragon
   vinegar
2 tablespoons prepared
   mustard
1 teaspoon salt
¼ teaspoon pepper

Mix all the vegetables.

Dressing: Combine dressing ingredients and mix well. Add dressing to vegetables.

Adeline Kohn

Celery Seed Dressing

1 teaspoon salt
1 teaspoon paprika
1 teaspoon celery seed
1 teaspoon prepared mustard
1 teaspoon grated onion

¼ cup vinegar
1 cup sugar
¼ cup olive oil
¼ cup salad oil

Combine all ingredients except oils in a blender or food processor; add oils gradually. Blend until thick. Let stand for 24 hours for flavors to mix before serving.

Yields 1¹/₄ cups.

JoAnne Rockower

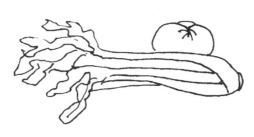

Asparagus Victor

2 pounds asparagus
14 ounces chicken broth
6 tablespoons olive oil
4 tablespoons white wine
   vinegar

2 tablespoons each finely
   chopped green onions and
   pimento
1 teaspoon Dijon mustard
salt and pepper, to taste

Break off white ends of asparagus. Wash well. In a large frying pan, heat broth to boiling. Lower the heat, add the asparagus and simmer 7 to 9 minutes or until tender. With tongs remove asparagus to a deep bowl. Save the broth for other uses. Blend together the remaining ingredients and pour over the asparagus. Cover and chill for 4 to 6 hours.

Cauliflower Salad

1 head fresh cauliflower, cut
   in small flowerettes
1/2 pound fresh mushrooms,
   sliced
1 cup ripe olives
1 green pepper, sliced
3 cloves garlic, mashed
2 tablespoons celery seed

juice of 2 lemons
hot pepper sauce, to taste
1 jar sliced pimentos
1 jar marinated artichokes
salt and pepper, to taste
1/2 teaspoon thyme
1/4 cup olive oil

Mix all ingredients together. Allow to marinate overnight and serve cold.

Judy Reibel

Dairy, Grains and Noodles

Sukkot

Every symbol and message of Sukkot cooperates to make the Jew conscious of the nature and world in which we live. Steeped in the agricultural origins of the people of biblical times, Sukkot also commemorates God's watchful care over the Israelites as they dwelt in frail huts during the forty years of wandering in the desert wilderness before entrance in the promised land. Sukkot is an ancestor of our American Thanksgiving. We give thanks for the blessing of the harvest and for God's miraculous production through the ages.

The holiday begins with the construction of a sukkah, a temporary arbor out in the garden or open space, followed by eight celebratory days of meals shared in the sukkah. The sukkah is decorated with cornstalks, gourds, pumpkins and children's pictures.

The lulav, a palm branch combined with myrtle and willow branches tied together, and the etrog, a lemon like citron, are the four festival symbols that may have been ancient talismans for rain, and represent different facets of the human body; the palm representing the spine, willow the eyes, myrtle the lips and the etrog the human heart.

Simchat Torah

Simchat Torah celebrates the completion of the yearly cycle of Torah readings, culminating in reading the last chapters of Deuteronomy and immediately starting the reading of the very first chapter of Genesis. The process of continuity of endings and beginnings is symbolized by the seven ceremonial processional circuits of congregants carrying as many Torahs and replicas as available. Simchat Torah procession originated in the 16th Century as a way of enabling children to feel closer to the Torah. Folklorists say that ceremonial circling was one of the oldest ways in which man used to try to appease the spirits; evil ones were thought to be kept out of the circle. It is customary to eat round foods to symbolize wholeness of the year. Today Israeli flags topped with apples are added to the procession.

What is...

BLINTZ is a filled pancake related to the Ukrainian blinchiki and the Russian blini. Blintzes were an everyday food of Central and Eastern European Jews, although the use of wheat flour and eggs meant that they were enjoyed more often by the well to do. In the United States today, the blintz is a paper-thin pancake made from a wheat flour and egg batter, folded up like a Chinese egg roll around a filling, cheese is the most common, and fried golden brown on both sides.

Quick Blintz Casserole

4 eggs, or equivalent
  substitute
1 pint sour cream
1 tablespoon vanilla
$1/2$ cup orange juice

2 packages frozen cheese or
  fruit blintzes
$1/2$ cup sugar, if using cheese
  blintzes
1 stick margarine

Melt margarine and pour into 9x13 inch pan. Lay blintzes on top of margarine. Mix eggs, sour cream, vanilla, orange juice and sugar (if making cheese blintzes). Pour mixture over blintzes. Bake at 375 degrees 50 minutes or until brown.

Elaine Halprin

Cheese Blintz

Pancakes:
4 eggs
1½ cups milk
¼ cup melted margarine
1 tablespoon sugar
1 cup flour

Filling:
1 pound cottage cheese
1 pound ricotta cheese
2 eggs
2 tablespoons sugar
2 tablespoons fresh lemon
  juice

Beat eggs and sugar together. Add flour, beat until smooth, thinning with a little milk to eliminate lumps. When batter is a smooth paste, add the rest of the milk slowly. Stir in the margarine. In a non-stick sauté pan, coat the bottom of the pan with a thin layer of batter. Flip over when edges are crispy and turn up easily. Set aside pancakes for filling.

Combine the filling ingredients. Place a heaping tablespoon of filling in each pancake, folding into little square pillows. Place pillows into a greased baking dish, cover with foil and bake at 350 degrees for 20 to 30 minutes. Serve with sour cream and fresh fruit or applesauce.

Makes 14 to 16 pancakes.

Diana Rosenthal

Blintz Soufflé

1/4 pound margarine, softened
1/3 cup sugar
6 eggs
1 1/2 cups dairy sour cream
1/2 cup orange juice
1 cup all-purpose flour
2 teaspoons baking powder

Blintz Filling:
1 (8 ounce) package cream
   cheese, cut up
2 cups small curd cottage
   cheese
2 egg yolks
1 tablespoon sugar
1 teaspoon vanilla extract

In a medium bowl or food processor fitted with a metal blade, combine all filling ingredients until blended.

Preheat oven to 350 degrees. Butter a 9x13 inch baking dish; set aside. In a blender, mix margarine, sugar, eggs, sour cream, orange juice, flour and baking powder until blended. Pour half the batter into a prepared baking dish. Drop filling by heaped spoonfuls over batter. With a knife, spread filling evenly. It will mix with the batter. Pour remaining batter over filling. Unbaked soufflé may be covered and refrigerated several hours or overnight until ready to use.

Before baking, bring soufflé to room temperature. Bake, uncovered 50 to 60 minutes or until puffed and golden. Serve immediately with sour cream and a blueberry syrup or assorted jams.

Makes 8 servings.

Lorraine Gerstl

Blueberry Stuffed "French Toast"

12 or more slices homemade
  style white bread
2 (8 ounce) packages non-fat
  cream cheese
2 cups blueberries
egg substitute to equal
  12 eggs

⅓ real maple syrup
2 cups non-fat milk
1 cup sugar
2 tablespoons cornstarch
1 cup water
1 tablespoon or more cognac

Cut crusts from bread and cut the bread into 1 inch cubes. Arrange half the bread cubes in a 9x13 inch glass baking dish sprayed with vegetable spray. Scatter cheese cut into 1 inch cubes over the bread and sprinkle 1 cup of blueberries over the cream cheese. Arrange the remaining bread cubes over the berries. In a large bowl whisk the egg substitute, syrup and milk and pour over the bread mixture evenly. Chill the mixture, covered overnight. Bake the "French Toast" covered with foil, in the middle of a preheated 350 degree oven for 30 minutes. Remove the foil and bake for 30 minutes more or until it is puffed and golden.

Sauce: In a small saucepan, stir together the sugar, cornstarch and water. Cook over moderate high heat, stirring occasionally for 5 minutes or until thickened. Stir in remaining berries and simmer for 10 minutes, stirring occasionally, until berries have burst. Add cognac and remove from stove.

Beth Weissman

Easy Egg Soufflé

16 slices white bread	6 eggs
3 (8 ounce) packages Old English grated cheddar cheese	1 teaspoon salt
	2 cups milk
	1 stick butter

Trim crusts from bread. Cut each slice into 4 sections. Beat eggs in bowl. Melt butter in a pan and set aside. Grease a 2 quart casserole. Layer bread on bottom and sides. Sprinkle cheese over that. Layer bread. Sprinkle cheese. Pour egg mixture over bread thoroughly and pour melted butter over top. Cover and place in refrigerator overnight.

When ready to use, place in oven. Put casserole in larger pan, in 1 inch of water. Keep covered. Put in oven at 400 degrees for 1½ hours.

Serves 12.

Judy Reibel

Puffy Omelette with Dill Sauce

4 egg whites	**Creamy Dill Sauce:**
2 egg yolks	½ cup cottage cheese
½ cup plain yogurt	¼ cup plain yogurt
salt and pepper, to taste	½ teaspoon dillweed
2 teaspoons butter	

Whip egg whites until stiff. Blend egg yolks, ½ cup yogurt, and salt and pepper to taste. Fold egg whites into yogurt mixture. Turn into buttered 9-inch skillet. Cover handle with aluminum foil if it is plastic or wood. Place on high rack in 350 degree oven and bake 15 to 20 minutes or until set. Run a spatula around edge of omelette to loosen. Slip onto serving platter, folding over in typical omelette fashion. (Omelette may crack a bit at the hinge because it is so thick.) Top with Creamy Dill Sauce.

Creamy Dill Sauce: Combine cottage cheese and ¼ cup yogurt in an electric blender container. Process until very smooth. Stir in dillweed. Chill before using.

Serves 2.

Barbara Taylor

What is...

KASHA *is the Russian name for buckwheat groats. In the past it was consumed so frequently that there arose a saying among the Russians that "buckwheat gruel is our mother and rye bread is our father."*

Kasha...Made Perfect

1 egg
1 cup kasha
¹/₄ cup margarine
1 cup chopped onion
1 cup chopped celery

2 cups warm chicken broth
¹/₄ teaspoon ground ginger
¹/₄ teaspoon dry mustard
salt

Combine the egg and kasha in a small bowl and set aside; sauté onion and celery in margarine in a large skillet. When tender, add kasha and stir over medium heat until each grain is separate. Add hot chicken broth, ginger, dry mustard; cover pan tightly and simmer for 15 minutes or until liquid is absorbed and grains are tender.

If you wish, you may add cooked bow-tie noodles; bell peppers, mushrooms...be creative! This is an excellent stuffing for turkey and/or chicken.

Deanna Adolph

Kasha Varnishkes

3 tablespoons olive oil
2 medium onions, sliced
¹/₂ pound fresh mushrooms

1 cup cooked kasha
2 cups cooked bow tie noodles
salt and pepper, to taste

Sauté onions and mushrooms in olive oil until soft. Add kasha and bow ties and heat in skillet to blend flavors. Season. Can be made a day or two in advance and reheated in the oven.

Barbara Lewit

Kasha Pilaf

1 cup commercially packaged
   kasha (buckwheat groats),
   medium grain if possible
1 egg
2 cups low-sodium canned
   chicken broth
½ teaspoon salt
¼ teaspoon pepper
1 tablespoon margarine

½ pound onions, coarsely
   chopped
3 tablespoons rendered
   chicken fat (or vegetable
   oil if desired)
½ pound button mushrooms,
   sliced
vegetable oil pan spray
salt and pepper, to taste

Cook the kasha, using the egg, chicken broth, salt, pepper, and only 1 tablespoon of margarine, following the procedure on the package. Fluff with a fork and set aside.

In a large non-stick skillet, sprinkle the chopped onions lightly with salt and pepper and sauté in the chicken fat (or vegetable oil) over medium heat until they are deep amber and very sweet. This must be done very slowly (may take up to 30 minutes), stirring frequently, to prevent the onions from burning. Set onions aside with any fat or oil remaining in the pan.

In a large non-stick skillet, sprinkle the sliced mushrooms lightly with salt and pepper and sauté in vegetable oil pan spray until most of their moisture has evaporated and they have become well browned, almost crispy. Set aside.

In a very large mixing bowl, toss together the cooled kasha, onions with their fat, mushrooms with their accumulated juices, with additional salt and pepper to taste, until well mixed. Transfer the pilaf to a casserole and reheat just before serving.

Makes 6 servings.

Karen Wiskoff

Orange Couscous Pilaf

1 cup orange juice	2 ounces dried currants
1/2 cup water	1 cup dry couscous grains
1/2 teaspoon salt	1 ounce sliced almonds
1 tablespoon margarine or butter	

Bring orange juice, water, salt, margarine or butter, and currants to a boil in a covered kettle. Remove from the heat and stir in the dry couscous. Cover and let stand 15 minutes; then fluff with a fork.

Reheat, if necessary, and stir in the almonds just before serving.

Makes 4 cups of pilaf.

Karen Wiskoff

Couscous Pilaf

2 cups boiling water, chicken or vegetable stock	1 red bell pepper, chopped
1 cup couscous	1 zucchini, chopped
1/2 teaspoon salt	1/2 cup cooked chickpeas
2 tablespoons olive oil	1/2 cup golden raisins
1 large onion, chopped	1/4 cup parsley, chopped
2 scallions, chopped	crushed red pepper, to taste

Combine water or broth and couscous and cover until all the liquid is absorbed, about 5 minutes. In a large skillet, heat oil. Add onion, scallions, bell pepper and zucchini and cook over medium heat until soft. Place in an oven-proof casserole dish and add remaining ingredients. Dot with margarine and bake for 20 minutes in a 350 degree oven.

Chile Relleno Puff

½ to 1 (4 ounce size) can
  California green chiles
6 eggs, separated
2 tablespoons flour
¾ teaspoon salt
⅛ teaspoon pepper

½ pound jack cheese,
  shredded or thinly sliced
1 (8 ounce) can tomato sauce
  with onion
2 tablespoons chopped
  parsley

Rinse the seeds from the chiles, pat dry, and cut in thin strips; set aside. Quantity of chiles varies depending on hotness desired. Beat the egg whites until they hold soft distinct peaks, then beat the egg yolks with flour, salt and pepper until thick and creamy. Fold the egg yolk mixture into the beaten whites. Spoon about ⅓ of the egg mixture into a greased 1½ quart souffle dish or other casserole. Over the eggs, arrange about half the chili strips and half of the cheese. Repeat these layers with another ⅓ of the egg mixture and remaining chiles and cheese. Top with remaining egg mixture.

Bake, uncovered, in a 350 degree oven for about 30 minutes, or until set in center. Meanwhile, combine the tomato sauce and parsley; simmer about 10 minutes. Serve tomato sauce separately to be spooned over each serving.

Serves 6.

JoAnne Rockower

Fried Rice

2 cups chopped cooked
  chicken
4 cups cooked rice
¼ cup oil
2 eggs, lightly beaten

2 tablespoons soy sauce
3 tablespoons chopped
  scallions
1 teaspoon salt

Sauté chicken in oil 1 minute. Add eggs, salt and pepper. Cook over medium heat for 5 minutes stirring. Add rice and soy sauce and cook another 5 minutes. Stir in scallions.

Judy Reibel

Kreplach

Dough:
2 cups flour
2 eggs
1½ teaspoons salt
1 tablespoon oil
Cheese Filling:
2 cups farmers or ricotta
   cheese
1 tablespoon sour cream

2 egg yolks
salt and pepper
Kasha Filling:
3 tablespoons chicken fat or
   butter
½ cup ground beef
⅔ cup minced onion
1½ cups cooked kasha

Sift flour and salt into a large bowl. Beat eggs with oil and add to the flour mixture. Knead until smooth. Divide dough in half. On well-floured board, roll out each half into a 12x14 inch rectangle. Cut into 3 inch squares.

Cheese Filling: Blend all ingredients together until well blended.

Kasha Filling: Heat fat or butter and fry onions and meat until pink is gone. Add kasha and spices and stir to blend well. Cool before filling.

Place 1 tablespoon of filling on each square. Brush edges with water, and fold into triangle, sealing all edges. Bring 2 corners together and press to seal, like a kerchief. To cook, drop into simmering salted water for 15 to 20 minutes, or fry in oil or margarine.

Makes about 40.

Bonni Weinstein

From age five to about ten or twelve, I ate only tuna, macaroni and cheese, and kreplach. Kreplach was my favorite, and I was the only grandchild who was permitted to help my Bubbe make them. When I was very young, I loved to eat the raw taig *(dough), and even though my Bubbe warned me that it would give me an upset stomach, she still slyly made an extra half recipe, so I could eat all I wanted and not mess up her serving calculations. Each year I got more and more nimble in my ability to shape the kreplach, until I was holding my own against the Bubbe, keeping up with her rapid pace. She loved to boast about my skillfulness, telling friends and family that I had* goldenah hentalach *(golden little hands). Those words have always stayed with me, and whenever I have doubts about my ability to do anything, I see her proudly beaming at me and hear her whispering "*goldenah hentalach.*" I know I can't possibly disappoint my Bubbe, so I just go ahead and do what needs to be done!*

Bonni Weinstein

Dried Fruit Stuffing

3½ cups chicken broth
1 cup dried apricots, coarsely
 chopped
4 tablespoons butter or
 margarine
1 cup diced yellow onion
1 cup diced celery
2 tart green apples, cored and
 cut into ½ inch cubes

1 tablespoon dried thyme
2 teaspoons rubbed sage,
 fresh if possible
1 teaspoon freshly ground
 black pepper
8 cups coarsely ground bread
 crumbs
2 cups shelled pecans
1 cup dried currants

Bring broth to a boil. Add apricots; remove from heat and let sit to plump. Heat butter or margarine in a large pan. Add diced onion and celery; cook, covered, over low heat for 10 minutes, stirring occasionally. Add broth, apricots, apple cubes, thyme, sage and pepper. Stir and transfer to a large bowl. Gradually add the bread crumbs, folding in gently until the stuffing is moist but not sticky. Mix in the pecans and currants. Let cool completely to room temperature before stuffing turkey.

This is enough for a 16-pound turkey.

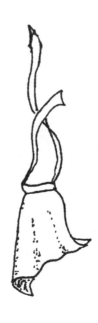

What is...

KUGEL, pudding, was a customary food on the Sabbath. Along with cholent, the kugel would be taken on Friday to a baker, who often was not Jewish, and collected the next day. The taking and collecting, which might be accomplished by the married women or by young unmarried men and women, was part of the social ritual of the community, serving as an opportunity for gossip or as a sort of youth club and marriage bureau. Today kugels are often made with noodles, dried fruits and eggs.

Lukshen Kugel

1½ red delicious apples, with skins
6 large eggs
3 teaspoons vanilla
¾ cup orange juice concentrate, undiluted
¾ cup seedless raisins
1½ cups chopped walnuts
1 cup sugar
2½ tablespoons ground cinnamon, or to taste
2 to 3 tablespoons ground fresh orange rind
20 ounces wide noodles
8 to 12 tablespoons unsalted butter

Grate apples into large mixing bowl. Add eggs and beat. Add vanilla, orange concentrate, raisins, walnuts, sugar, cinnamon and orange rind. Mix well. Cook noodles according to package instructions and drain well. Add noodles to above mixture and gently stir to mix. Using 2 pans, if necessary, coat glass baking dish, iron skillet or pan with half the melted butter. Pour kugel mixture into pans and dot with remaining butter. Bake at 350 degrees on bottom oven shelf for 45 to 55 minutes for larger pans and 30 to 35 minutes for smaller pans.

Margye Neswitz

Sweet and Tender Noodles

½ pound broad egg noodles
1 pound cottage cheese
½ pint sour cream
4 eggs, room temperature and separated

¼ cup sugar
1 teaspoon vanilla
⅛ teaspoon cream of tartar
4 tablespoons butter

Preheat oven to 350 degrees. Cook noodles as directed on package. While noodles cook, process cottage cheese, sour cream, egg yolks, sugar and vanilla. Set aside. Beat egg whites until foamy. Add cream of tartar and continue beating until whites stand in peaks. Drain noodles and mix with butter. Stir in cheese mixture, blending completely. Fold in egg whites and spread in buttered 9x13 inch glass baking dish. Bake for 50 to 60 minutes, or until noodles are lightly browned on top.

Serves 6.

Barbara Taylor

Long before I knew the difference between my German grandmother's cooking and Jewish cooking, I loved her sweet noodles. Everyone who tasted this glorious dish begged for the recipe. She didn't have a recipe because she knew how to make it. I watched her and eventually was able to recreate its light, fluffy texture.

It wasn't until I moved to Baltimore that I discovered what the noodle recipe really was. My Jewish neighbor who delighted in sharing her kitchen secrets with a young bride, asked me "where did you learn to make kugel?" I told her about Gramma. Before coming to America from Lithuania, she learned all about keeping a kosher kitchen while living with a Jewish doctor's family. Although Gramma faithfully attended church each Sunday until shortly before her death, her kitchen, nevertheless, had all the wonderful aromas of a Jewish Bubbe's kitchen.

Barbara Taylor

Noodle Kugel

1 cup white raisins
$1/2$ cup sweet white wine
8 ounces narrow egg noodles
3 eggs, beaten well
$1/4$ pound butter
1 teaspoon cinnamon

8 ounces soft cream cheese
1 cup sour cream
1 cup milk
$3/4$ cup sugar
1 teaspoon vanilla

Soak raisins in white wine 4 hours or overnight. Boil noodles; drain. Add butter to drained noodles. Add all other ingredients. Pour into oblong glass baking dish. Bake, 350 degrees 1 hour or until top is brown.

Ronnie Zipper

Thin Noodle Kugel

$1/2$ pound "fine" noodles
8 extra large eggs
$1/2$ cup sugar
2 teaspoons vanilla
8 ounces cream cheese

$1/2$ pound butter
1 pint sour cream
Topping:
1 cup graham cracker crumbs
1 stick butter, melted

Cook and drain noodles. Beat eggs a little first, then beat in other ingredients and blend in noodles. Mix the topping ingredients. Sprinkle a little of the topping on the bottom of a 9x13 inch pan. Pour in noodle mixture and top with the rest of the crumbs. Bake at 350 degrees for 1 hour.

Kerry Beren

Yom Tov Kugel

3 eggs, well beaten
1/4 cup sugar
1 teaspoon cinnamon
1/4 teaspoon nutmeg
1/2 cup orange juice
1 tablespoon grated orange
    rind
1 tablespoon grated lemon
    rind

1 (9 ounce) package wide
    noodles, cooked and
    drained
1/2 cup melted margarine
1 cup apple diced
1/2 cup diced dried apricots
1/2 cup slivered almonds
1/2 cup white raisins
1/4 cup matzo meal

Beat eggs with sugar, cinnamon and nutmeg. Stir in juice, and rinds. Pour mixture over cooked noodles and combine with melted margarine. Combine apples, apricots, nuts and raisins. Oil a 2 1/2 or 3 quart baking dish and layer half of noodle mixture, then fruit mixture and remaining noodles. Sprinkle top with matzo meal and dot with 2 tablespoons margarine. Bake in 350 degree oven for 1 hour or until golden brown.

Serves 6 to 8.

Chanukah Noodle Kugel

12 ounces egg noodles, wide
1/2 cup sugar
2 tablespoons sugar
1/2 cup soft butter
1 cup sour cream
1 cup cottage cheese
4 eggs, beaten
1 teaspoon vanilla

2 teaspoons cinnamon
5 ounces frozen orange juice
    concentrate, undiluted,
    thawed (leave 1 ounce off
    can)
1 apple, large cooking, cut
    into small pieces
raisins, optional

Cook noodles, drain, toss with 1/2 cup sugar. Mix together butter, sour cream, cottage cheese, eggs, vanilla, cinnamon, orange juice and raisins. Stir in apple and noodles. Turn into 9x13 inch greased pan. Sprinkle with remaining 2 tablespoons of sugar. Bake at 350 degrees for 50 minutes. Enjoy!

Serves 10.

Andrea Carter

Rita's Delicious Noodle Kugel

1 pound wide egg noodles,
   cooked and drained
1 pound regular cream
   cheese, softened
1½ cups sugar
8 ounces margarine, melted

8 eggs
4 cups whole milk
1 cup crushed corn flakes
cinnamon and sugar, mixed
   to taste

Whip cream cheese with an electric mixer. Whip in sugar, followed by margarine, eggs, and milk, one at a time. The mixture will be thin.

Place cooked noodles in a greased 9x13 inch baking pan. Pour the cream cheese mixture over the noodles and refrigerate overnight, covered with waxed paper or aluminum foil. The kugel will congeal.

When ready to bake kugel, preheat oven to 350 degrees. Before baking, sprinkle top with crushed corn flakes and cinnamon/sugar mixture to taste. Bake until set, about 70 minutes. Let kugel cool slightly before cutting.

24 portions.

Karen Wiskoff

Lee's Noodle Kugel

1 pound medium noodles
2 tablespoons melted
   margarine
6 eggs (or equivalent of 6 egg
   substitute)
1 (15 ounce) can unsweetened
   applesauce

½ cup milk (regular, low fat
   on non-fat)
white raisins (or cut up dried
   fruit bits)
cinnamon and sugar, to taste

Cook noodles according to package directions, drain and rinse, and toss with the melted margarine. Beat the eggs, add the applesauce, sugar, milk and raisins. Mix all the ingredients together and pour into a greased 2 quart baking dish. Bake at 375 degrees for 1 hour.

Linda Kaiser

Noodle Kugel

1 (12 ounce) package wide egg
  noodles
2 peeled, sliced apples
1 package dried apricots
1 cup raisins
1 can crushed pineapple
  (with juice)
³/₄ cup sugar
cinnamon
8 ounces cream cheese

8 ounces sour cream
8 ounces cottage cheese
1 stick of butter
Topping:
3 eggs
2 cups milk
¹/₂ stick butter
1 cup corn flake crumbs
¹/₂ cup sugar
more cinnamon

Cook noodles until tender; drain. Mix all fruit, sugar and cinnamon and set aside. Add cream cheese, sour cream, cottage cheese and butter to warm noodles. Mix well. Add fruit mixture to noodle mixture and blend well. Pour into 9x13 inch pan.

Topping: Beat 3 eggs. Add 2 cups milk and heat until warm. Pour over noodle/fruit mixture. Melt ¹/₂ stick butter in a pan and brown corn flake crumbs, sugar and cinnamon. Sprinkle over the top. Bake 1¹/₄ hours at 375 degrees.

Eda Kunitz

Low-Fat Kugel

12 ounce package cholesterol
  free egg noodle substitute
16 ounce container, low fat
  cottage cheese
1¹/₄ cups egg substitute
  (equivalent of 5 eggs)
¹/₂ cup milk
1 green apple, chopped

¹/₄ cup dried apricots,
  chopped
¹/₄ cup raisins
¹/₂ teaspoon cinnamon
¹/₄ cup brown sugar
2 teaspoons grated orange
  rind (optional)

Cook noodles according to package directions. Drain. Combine all other ingredients. Mix well. Add drained noodles and mix. Spray 9x13 inch glass or metal baking pan with a non-stick pan spray or lightly oil the pan. Pour in mixture. Bake, uncovered at 350 degrees for approximately 45 minutes, or until lightly browned on top. Serve warm or at room temperature. Cut into squares to serve.

Serves 8.

Barbara Mitchell

Heart's Delight
Lukshen Kugel

8 ounces no yolk, wide
  noodles
1 teaspoon vanilla
1/4 pound non-fat cream
  cheese
1/2 pint non-fat sour cream
4 egg whites, or the
  equivalent of 2 egg
  substitutes
6 1/2 ounce can crushed
  pineapple in water

2 tablespoons fructose
1/2 cup raisins
1 teaspoon salt
Topping:
1 cup non-sugar flakes
  (Nutrigrain or other)
1 teaspoon cinnamon
1 tablespoon fructose

Cook noodles according to package directions. Drain and rinse under hot water. Return to cooking pan which has been sprayed with non-stick cooking spray. Add cream cheese, cut in 1 inch squares, and remaining ingredients. Mix well and put in 8x8 inch pan lined with foil and sprayed with non-stick cooking spray. Refrigerate overnight. Top with corn flake topping before baking for 1 hour at 350 degrees.

Topping: Blend 1 cup non-sugar flakes, 1 teaspoon cinnamon and 1 tablespoon fructose until finely crumbled. Shredded wheat or Grapenuts work well, too.

This recipe is an adaptation of my sister-in-law, Sara's, fabulous kugel. Its secret lies in the overnight refrigeration, which marinates the noodles in the cheese mixture until every noodle is soaked with flavor.

Bonni Weinstein

Great California Kugel

8 ounces medium noodles
1³/₄ cups warm milk
³/₄ cup sugar
3 eggs
6 ounces cream cheese

¼ pound melted butter
1 pint sour cream
1¹/₂ teaspoons vanilla
¼ teaspoon salt

Mix cooked noodles, milk and sugar and set aside. Put remaining ingredients in blender and blend together. Add 1 cup raisins and pour over noodle mixture. Put in a 3 quart well greased pan. Sprinkle with sugar and cinnamon. Bake at 350 degrees for 1 hour.

Serves 8 to 12.

JoAnne Rockower

Noodle Pudding Soufflé

3 eggs, separated
1 stick butter, melted
2 tablespoons sugar
1 pound creamed cottage
   cheese

1 cup sour cream
¹/₂ pound medium noodles
¹/₂ cup corn flakes, crushed
butter

Cook noodles and drain. Beat egg yolks; add melted butter and sugar. Fold in the cottage cheese, sour cream and noodles. Fold in stiffly beaten egg whites. Place in a 2 quart buttered casserole and sprinkle the top with crushed corn flakes. Dot generously with butter. Bake 45 minutes in a 375 degree oven.

Serves 8.

Adeline Kohn

Vegetables & Potatoes

Hanukkah

Hanukkah, the festival of rededication, is an eight day festival occurring during the month of December. It commemorates the rededication of the Second Temple in 165 B.C.E. when against all odds, a small group of Jews overcame the mighty Syrian oppressors who sought to obliterate Jewish belief and convert all Jews to the way of Hellenism. When the victory was achieved, the immediate concern was to purify the Temple and reconsecrate the altar for the renewal to daily services. The lovely story, if not necessarily based on traceable fact, is that when cleansing the Temple only one undefiled vial of oil for burning in the menorah could be found. Through a miracle this lasted for not one day but eight. In commemoration of this miracle, the festival is celebrated for eight days. Lights are burned in a special eight branched menorah beginning with one light and adding one each night.

Hanukkah is a festival primarily celebrated in the home, with the lighting and blessing of the menorah candles, eating of foods cooked in oil, such as latkes or jelly filled donuts. Some say it takes a whole year to recover from the cholesterol overload. The playing of a game with a spinning top called Dreidl, singing, children's plays and the giving of gifts are all part of the holiday.

Zucchini Pancakes

4 medium zucchini	1 stalk of celery
1 medium potato	2 eggs
1 carrot	1 medium onion

Grate all vegetables. Drain any excess liquid. Add eggs and blend well. Add salt, garlic powder and pepper, some diced chives and dried celery leaves. Add enough matzo meal to be firm enough to make a pancake in the palm of your hand. Heat olive oil, add pancakes and brown on both sides. Place on a paper towel to absorb excess oil. Can be served hot or cold.

Anna Shelkowsky

Tirtsa's Carrots

carrots	1 clove garlic, mashed or
1 tablespoon margarine	minced
1/2 teaspoon cumin	salt and pepper
1 teaspoon sugar	

Peel, slice and boil carrots until tender. Drain and set aside. Melt margarine in pan and add cumin, sugar and garlic. Sauté a minute and return carrots to pan, tossing to coat with sauce. Season to taste.

Diana Rosenthal

Carrot Ring

1/2 cup brown sugar	1/2 teaspoon baking powder
1 cup corn oil	1/2 teaspoon baking soda
2 eggs separated, beat whites	pinch of salt (optional)
1 cup grated carrots	2 tablespoons water
1 1/4 cups flour	

Mix above. Fold in egg whites. Bake in greased ring or loaf pan at 350 degrees for 40 minutes.

This is one of Rabbi Greenbaum's favorites!

Susan Greenbaum

When I was growing up, every Sunday after Religious School, my family would drive to my Aunt Lil's, to pay our respects to my Bubbe and her sister, Tante Zlota. My mother's other sister would also drive, with her family to converge on my Aunt's for the afternoon. My Aunt Lil would cook for days for these visits, and everyone in the family agreed that she was the maven of the kitchen in our family. She served the men herring and chopped liver and every uncle knew where the schnapps was kept. She served the children sweet noshes, which we took up to the third floor landing to enjoy while we did homework. The women stayed in the kitchen, kibitzing, finishing each others' sentences and discussing the fate of their lives. Tante Zlota often stayed in her apartment on the third floor. She spoke mostly Yiddish and she seemed severe, though my mother says this is not true. She always had a box of prunes to give us, and a pat on the head. My Bubbe was more approachable. She let us confide our secrets to her, and by her bedside was a sugar bowl full of packaged sugar cubes, which she doled out to us one by one. My Aunt Lil never wrote her recipes down and she is gone now. Once in a while, I come across a sugar cube, however, and those wonderful Sunday afternoons come flooding back.

Ginny Rosenberg

Yams Gratin

4 cups apricot nectar
1 cup chicken broth
6 tablespoons unsalted
   margarine or butter
1/2 cup chopped dried apricots

salt to taste
1/2 teaspoon cinnamon
1/2 teaspoon pepper
5 1/2 pounds long orange yams

Peel and slice yams into 1/8 inch thick slices. Mix together all but the yams and heat until the margarine or butter melts. Add the yams and bring to a boil. Reduce heat, cover and cook about 15 minutes until the yams are soft. Transfer the yams with slotted spoon to a glass baking dish. Pour the juices over them and press down to compact. Cover with foil and bake 30 minutes in a 400 degree oven. Uncover and continue to bake about 55 minutes or until tender and browned. Let set for 15 minutes before serving. This is a terrific dish for a dairy pot luck.

Kerry Beren

Sweet-Sour Red Cabbage

1 tablespoon butter or
   margarine
1/2 cup wine vinegar
1/4 cup honey

1 teaspoon salt
1 medium head (8 cups) red
   cabbage, shredded
2 apples, cored and diced

Melt butter in large non-stick skillet over medium heat. Stir in vinegar, honey and salt. Add cabbage and apples; toss well. Reduce heat to low; cover and simmer 45 to 50 minutes.

To microwave: Place shredded cabbage in 3 quart microwave safe baking dish. Add apples, butter and vinegar. Cover and cook on high for 15 minutes. Stir in honey and salt. Cover and cook on high 10 minutes.

Serves 4 to 6.

Barbara Taylor

Mom's Savory Eggplant

2 pounds eggplant
1/4 cup flour
oil for frying
2 onions, finely chopped

1 cup tomato sauce
1/4 cup seasoned bread crumbs
salt and ginger, to taste
3 tablespoons margarine

Slice unpared eggplant crosswise. Dip in a little flour and fry in oil until browned on both sides. Fry in small batches. To lower fat content, broil eggplant until tender after spraying with light vegetable oil cooking spray. Chop or mash cooked eggplant. Add onions, tomato sauce, crumbs, salt and fresh chopped or powdered ginger to taste. Arrange in oiled small casserole. Dot with margarine or butter and sprinkle on a few bread crumbs. Bake 30 minutes at 350 degrees or until browned on top.

Pauline Thomas

What a baalaboste my mother, Shirley Cotell, was! She is remembered for her wonderful cooking as well as her wonderfully warm, giving and uncomplicated nature. My mother was the little aproned Jewish Mama from Poland and a culinary adventurer as well. My father, on the other hand, was wary of uncharted territory when it came to food and considered any vegetable other than green beans exotic. However, when it came to this dish, he forgot to complain.

Pauline Thomas

Oven-Roasted Eggplant

¹/₄ cup seasoned bread crumbs
¹/₄ cup fresh grated Parmesan
   cheese

1 medium eggplant
¹/₂ cup olive oil
garlic and oregano, to taste

Preheat oven to 375 degrees. Slice the eggplant into ¹/₄ inch slices. Line baking sheet with foil. Combine bread crumbs, cheese and seasonings. Toss eggplant in oil and roll in breadcrumb mixture. Place on baking sheet and bake 15 to 20 minutes or until crisp.

Joyce Kurtz

Berenjena (Fried Eggplant)

1 eggplant, large peeled and
   sliced
¹/₂ teaspoon salt
pepper, to taste
¹/₂ cup flour
1 to 2 eggs, beaten

oil, for frying
Sauce:
¹/₂ cup tomato sauce
¹/₂ cup water
¹/₂ teaspoon sugar
1 clove garlic, chopped

Soak eggplant in salt water. Drain well and dry slices. Dip in seasoned flour then into beaten eggs. Brown well on each side in preheated oil. Drain well on paper towels. Place slices in sauce in baking pan in 350 degree oven for 30 minutes.

Esther Stern

White Onions Baked in Honey

3 large white onions
  (about 3 pounds)
1/3 cup honey
1/4 cup water
3 tablespoons butter or
  margarine, melted

1 teaspoon sweet Hungarian
  paprika
1 teaspoon ground coriander
1/2 teaspoon salt
1/8 teaspoon ground red
  pepper

Peel onions and cut crosswise into halves. Place cut side down in shallow baking dish just large enough to hold all onions in a single layer. Sprinkle with water; cover with foil. Bake at 350 degrees 30 minutes. Combine honey, 1/4 cup water, butter, paprika, coriander, salt and red pepper in small bowl. Remove onions from the oven and turn cut side up. Spoon half of mixture over onions. Bake, uncovered, 15 minutes more. Baste with remaining honey mixture; bake 15 minutes more or until tender.

Serves 6.

Barbara Taylor

Delicious Asparagus

2 packages frozen asparagus
1 can cream of mushroom soup

1 package sliced Swiss cheese

Cook asparagus according to directions. Drain. Place in oven proof dish. Mix soup in and place Swiss cheese on top and cover completely. Bake at 350 degrees for 15 minutes or until cheese is completely melted. Can be made in advance and reheated.

Judy Reibel

Oven-Roasted Vegetables

1 pound new potatoes	2 tablespoons olive or canola
1 pound yams	oil
3 large carrots	1 tablespoon chopped fresh or
2 medium onions	1 teaspoon dried thyme
1 large red pepper	1 tablespoon chopped fresh or
1 large green pepper	1 teaspoon dried oregano
1 bunch radishes	

Preheat oven to 400 degrees. Cut new potatoes into 1 inch pieces. Peel yams; cut into 1 inch pieces. Cut carrots into 1 inch pieces. Cut onions into ½ inch wedges. Cut green and red peppers into 1 inch pieces. Trim edges from radishes.

In roasting pan toss vegetables with oil and herbs. Roast 1 hour until vegetables are tender, stirring occasionally.

Serves 6.

Barbara Taylor

Broccoli Casserole

1 bunch broccoli	¼ teaspoon pepper
½ cup chopped onion	2 eggs
2 tablespoons margarine or	2 cups milk
butter	2 cups cooked brown rice
1 teaspoon salt	1½ cups grated cheese

Cook and chop broccoli. Sauté onion in margarine or butter. Add everything. Bake in buttered casserole at 325 degrees for 1¼ hours.

Kerry Beren

Fritada de Tomat

2 (14 ounce) cans stewed
   tomatoes
½ teaspoon sugar
2 slices soft bread crumbs
1 tablespoon oil

¼ pound feta cheese, crumbled
4 eggs, well beaten
1 cup grated Parmesan or
   Romano cheese
½ cup chopped parsley

Heat oil in pan. Add tomatoes, mash them and simmer until tomatoes are thick. Add remaining ingredients. Mix well. Pour into greased 6x9 inch or 8x8 inch baking dish. Bake in 425 degree oven for 30 to 35 minutes until brown on top.

Esther Stern

Baked Okra

1 pound fresh or frozen okra
2 tablespoons canola oil
2 medium onions, chopped
4 medium tomatoes, peeled
   and cut in small pieces
   or 1 (16 ounce) can tomatoes

½ teaspoon salt,
   less if using canned
   tomatoes
1 tablespoon lemon juice

Combine all ingredients in saucepan, bring to boil, cover and simmer on low until tender. Put in a shallow baking dish and bake uncovered at 375 degrees for 45 to 60 minutes or until browned.

Serves 4.

Ethel Alvy

Quick Party Soufflé

3 whole eggs
3 heaping tablespoons
   mayonnaise
½ cup canned white sauce

1 package frozen vegetables
   (corn, chopped spinach,
   chopped broccoli are best)
salt and pepper

Mix all ingredients in a blender or food processor at high speed. Pour into an ungreased 1½ quart soufflé dish and bake for approximately 1 hour at 350 degrees or until center rises in a crown.

Serves 4 generously.

JoAnne Rockower

Stuffed Baked Potatoes

1 package frozen chopped
    spinach, defrosted
    (chopped broccoli may be
    used)
3 large russet baking
    potatoes, baked well

¼ cup canola oil
2 tablespoons dried onion
    flakes
1 cup grated cheese (your
    choice, low-fat cheese may
    be used)

Cut the baked potatoes length-wise, scoop them out and mash with the oil, onion flakes, salt to taste, and cheese. Stir spinach in potato mixture. Stuff the mixture back into the shells, sprinkle tops with paprika and bake in a preheated 350 degree oven for 20 to 30 minutes.

Served with a salad, these potatoes make a great vegetarian dinner.

Serves 2.

Shelly Glaser

Potatoes Lilly

potatoes
onions
apples

butter
seasonings

Peel and slice potatoes, onions and apples. You may use a food processor. Grease a pan and begin with a layer of onions, topped by a layer of apples and then the potatoes. Keep layering until the pan is nearly full. Dot with butter and season to taste. Bake in a 375 degree oven until done and the top has browned.

Shortly before she died Freda Peck gave us this recipe to put in the cookbook. It is a variation of her sister, Lilly Trube's recipe that was in our previous cookbook *So Come to the Table*. Since there are no measurements of ingredients, use your imagination and enjoy a good vegetarian side dish.

What is...

LATKES are potato pancakes, a common food of Lithuanian Jews, who made them from grated potatoes fried in poppy seed oil or fat. Jews in the Ukraine and other Eastern European regions were accustomed to eating buckwheat latkes instead. Fried latkes are popular at Hanukkah because of the association of fried foods with the miracle of the oil.

Blender Potato Latkes

3 eggs
5 or 6 medium sized potatoes
3 slices onions
2 large sprigs of parsley

$^1/_3$ cup unsifted flour
$^1/_4$ teaspoon baking powder
$1^1/_2$ teaspoons salt

Scrub potatoes carefully and cut into 1 inch cubes. Break eggs into blender container and blend. Add vegetables a few at a time and blend until they are cut fine. Add baking powder and salt and blend just to mix. Fry in oil in a hot skillet or on a hot greased griddle. Serve with applesauce and/or sour cream.

JoAnne Rockower

Potato Latkes

4 large potatoes
    (or 6 medium)
1 small onion
2 eggs

$^1/_8$ teaspoon baking powder
$^1/_2$ teaspoon salt
1 tablespoon flour
dash pepper

Grate potatoes with onion, by hand or blender. Drain excess water. Add eggs, flour, salt and pepper. Mix well. Fry in hot oil, turning when golden brown. Drain on paper towel before serving. Serve with applesauce, sugar, cinnamon or sour cream.

Larry Solow

Lester's Grandmother's Latkes

5 pounds potatoes
3 large eggs
2 to 3 handfuls matzo meal

salt, pepper and garlic
   powder, to taste
onion
oil

Lester's Grandmother cooked the way all our grandmothers cooked, with handsful and pinches, so enjoy getting your hands into this recipe!

Peel potatoes and coarsely grate into small bits (not the shoestring type of grating). Let drain to get rid of the potato liquid. Add eggs and 2 to 3 handfuls of matzo meal (Lester says: "I'm sorry but this is the only way I can do this"). Add salt, pepper and garlic powder to taste. Grate onion directly into the potato mixture as you want the onion juice. You know you have the batter correct if it sticks to your fingers as it drips through. Get your pan hot with a good layer of oil and throw out the first three latkes you make because the oil is never hot enough.

Lester Tockerman

Quick Knishes

1 package Pepperidge Farm
   puff pastry

mashed potatoes

Roll puff pastry in rectangle and spread with your favorite mashed potato recipe seasoned with minced onions. Roll jelly roll fashion, slice and bake in a 375 degree oven until well browned.

Judy Levine

Aunt Dorothy's
Mashed Potato Knishes

8 large potatoes, boiled and
   mashed
2 eggs
1 teaspoon baking powder
1/4 to 3/4 cup flour

1 large onion, chopped
2 cups cooked meat or
   poultry
salt and pepper

Add 1 egg and baking powder to mashed potato. Then add flour a little at a time until the mixture is easy to handle and does not stick to fingers. To make the filling, sauté onion in oil until tender; add the chopped cooked meat and warm through. Remove from heat, add seasonings and 1 egg to bind. Take a small handful of the potato mixture, cup it in your hand and add a heaping tablespoon of the filling. Fold the potato mixture around the filling, covering it completely. Bake on a greased baking sheet at 350 degrees for 1 hour, or until brown.

Bonni Weinstein

Swiss Potatoes

1 1/2 pounds big baking
   potatoes, sliced thin
1 teaspoon salt
1 teaspoon minced dried
   onions

2 eggs, beaten
1 1/2 cups scalded milk
1/4 pound grated Swiss
   cheese

Mix all of the above ingredients in a medium size baking dish; and sprinkle top with more cheese. Bake uncovered at 350 degrees for 1 hour or at 300 degrees for 1 hour and 15 minutes.

JoAnne Rockower

Entrées

Tu B'Shvat

Jewish Arbor Day is known as the New Year of the trees and is a day for planting of trees. The holiday has its origin in ancient spring agricultural celebrations and one custom that has come down through the ages is the tasting of at least fifteen different types of fruits. The number is chosen because the holiday occurs on the fifteenth day of the month and occurs in January or February. A large variety of fruits, dried, fresh and in baked goods are usually served.

Purim

The story of the biblical Book of Esther is the merriest of Jewish festivals. Purim celebrates a reversal of Jewish persecution. Though the actual events in the Persian site are clouded in antiquity and may never have actually happened, the message was considered so extremely important to be included when the Bible was being codified. Purim is celebrated with costumed parties and merry rereading of the Book of Esther complete with cheering and booing by the participants. Hamantaschen, triangular shaped filled cookies, are associated with Purim. The first written mention of the poppy seed honey mixture in connection with Purim is found in a medieval poem by Abraham Ibn Ezra, who lived in the early part of the twelfth century. The choice of filling is yours, whether poppy seed, fruit or prune.

Shabbat Roast Chicken

1 chicken, cut up
  (or equivalent pieces —
  much easier)
3 yellow onions, chopped
3 cloves garlic, minced

salt or garlic salt, to taste
pepper
paprika
sliced mushrooms
  (optional)

Wash and pat dry chicken pieces. Place chopped onion, garlic and mushrooms in layer on bottom of roasting pan. Sprinkle with pepper and plenty of paprika. Lay chicken pieces out on top of onions. Dust with salt, pepper and paprika. Preheat oven to 325 degrees. Cover roasting pan. Place in oven 50 to 60 minutes. Remove lid and continue roasting 10 to 15 minutes until chicken is browned. Serve with onions and juice as gravy.

Kris Orliss

Chicken Fricassee

1 stewing chicken
3 large onions, diced
1 tablespoon corn oil

garlic salt, salt and pepper,
  to taste
flour (to thicken)

Cut chicken into small pieces at the joint. Brown in the corn oil, add onions, garlic salt, salt and pepper and sauté until light brown. When browned add 1 cup of water. Sprinkle lightly with flour; cover and simmer until chicken is tender (2½ hours). If liquid dries out, add more water.

Judy Reibel

Honey Chicken

4 to 5 pounds whole chickens,
  each cut into 4 or 8 pieces
seasoned flour (salt, pepper,
  garlic, paprika, to taste)

1 egg
1 tablespoon lemon juice
3 tablespoons margarine
7 ounces honey

Beat egg and lemon juice. Dip chicken pieces in flour, then into egg and brown in margarine until golden. Place in casserole dish and spoon honey over chicken. Bake at 350 degrees for 45 to 60 minutes, until dark golden.

Carol Gross

Apricot Glazed Chicken

1 roasting chicken (4 to 5
  pounds)
1 cup seedless red or green
  grapes
4 tablespoons honey, divided
1 (16 ounce) can apricot
  halves, divided

¼ cup butter or margarine,
  melted
2 teaspoons seasoned salt
¼ teaspoon pepper
½ cup dry white wine or
  chicken broth
grape clusters and fresh
  herbs for garnish

Rinse chicken in cold water and pat dry with paper towels. Toss 1 cup grapes with 2 tablespoons of honey into small bowl. Place grapes in body cavity. Tie legs close to body and fold wing tips back or secure with skewers or cotton string. Place chicken, breast side up, on rack in roasting pan.

Drain apricot halves, reserving syrup. Set aside 6 halves for garnish. Puree remaining apricots in blender or food processor with melted butter, seasoned salt, pepper and remaining 2 tablespoons of honey. Brush over chicken. Pour wine and ¼ cup apricot syrup in bottom of pan. Cover chicken loosely with tented foil.

Roast at 350 degrees 1¾ to 2 hours or until chicken is tender and thermometer inserted in thigh registers 180 degrees. Baste occasionally with pan drippings to glaze. Remove foil during last 30 minutes of roasting. Serve chicken on platter garnished with clusters of grapes, apricot halves and fresh herbs.

Serves 6 to 8.

Barbara Davis Taylor

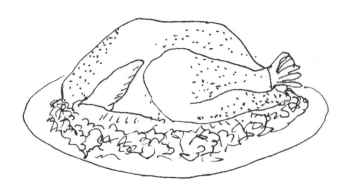

Good Yom Tov Chicken

2 broiler-fryer chickens,
large, cut up
1 cup matzo meal
1 teaspoon salt
1 dash pepper
1/2 cup peanut oil
2 cups onions, chopped

1 cup dried figs, sliced
(about 8 ounces)
4 cups applesauce
1 teaspoon cinnamon
1 cup blanched almonds,
slivered
1 cup orange juice
2 teaspoons orange rind

Roll chicken parts in mixture of matzo meal, salt and pepper. Fry in hot oil in large skillet until brown on both sides. Remove from pan. Drain off all but 2 tablespoons fat. Add onions; cook until tender. Return chicken to pan. Scatter fig slices around chicken. Mix applesauce, orange juice and rind and cinnamon. Pour over chicken and figs. Cover for 30 minutes or until tender. Add almonds. Cook 5 minutes.

Serves 6 to 8.

Maxine Suval

Chicken Bernardino

1 chicken, cut up
3 tablespoons salad oil
1 (8 ounce) can tomato sauce
1/2 cup sherry

1/3 cup orange marmalade
1/4 cup chopped onions
1 tablespoon Worcestershire
sauce

Sauté chicken in oil. Mix remaining ingredients and pour on chicken. Bake 325 degrees for 45 minutes.

Serves 4.

Joyce Kurtz

Soy-Honey Chicken

½ cup soy sauce
½ cup honey
¼ cup dry sherry or apple
   juice
1 teaspoon grated fresh
   ginger root

2 medium cloves garlic,
   crushed
1 broiler-fryer chicken,
   cut into serving pieces
   (2½ to 3 pounds)

Combine soy sauce, honey, sherry, ginger root and garlic in a small bowl. Place chicken into zip-lock plastic food bag or large glass baking dish. Pour honey marinade over chicken, turning to coat. Close bag or cover dish with plastic wrap. Marinate in refrigerator at least 6 hours, turning two or three times.

Remove chicken from marinade; reserve marinade. Arrange chicken on rack over roasting pan. Cover chicken with foil. Bake at 350 degrees for 30 minutes. Bring reserved marinade to a boil in small saucepan over medium heat; boil 3 minutes and set aside.

Uncover chicken; brush with marinade. Bake, uncovered 30 to 45 minutes longer or until juices run clear and chicken is no longer pink, brushing occasionally with marinade.

Substitute 2 teaspoons ground ginger for fresh ginger root, if desired.

Serves 4.

Barbara Taylor

Chicken Casserole with Prunes

¹/₄ cup vegetable oil
3 cups sliced onions
2 tablespoons flour
2 frying chickens, cut up

salt and pepper
1 pound prunes
2 (8 ounce) cans tomato sauce

This recipe is very easy to put together; no browning of the chicken is necessary. It has won runner-up in two cooking contests!

Put oil in deep 3 quart casserole. Add onions and sprinkle flour over onions. Put half the chicken pieces on onions; sprinkle with salt and pepper. Add ¹/₂ the prunes and 1 cup tomato sauce. Repeat layers of chicken, prunes and seasonings. Pour remaining sauce over the top. Cover and bake in a 350 degree oven for about 2 hours.

Barbara Lewit

Chicken and Artichokes

1 chicken cut up in pieces
1 can artichoke hearts
¹/₄ cup mushrooms, quartered
3 tablespoons minced onions
oil for cooking

salt, pepper and paprika
2 tablespoons flour
²/₃ cups chicken broth
¹/₄ cup sherry
¹/₂ teaspoon rosemary

Brown chicken in butter or oil. Remove from pan to baking dish and top with artichoke hearts. Brown mushrooms and onions and when cooked add to chicken-artichoke baking dish. Sprinkle flour in frying pan and add remaining ingredients, scraping pan. Cook a few minutes and add to other ingredients. Bake in a 375 degree oven for 40 minutes.

Serves 4.

Joyce Kurtz

Curry Chicken

1 whole chicken, cut up (or
  your favorite parts)
1 cup honey

¹/₂ cup mustard (all-American,
  ballpark variety)
curry, to taste

In a small saucepan, heat honey and mustard until bubbling. Add curry. Pour the sauce over the chicken and bake at 375 degrees for 1 to 1¹/₄ hours. Turn chicken once or twice while baking.

Joyce Kurtz

Chicken Marengo

1 large onion, thinly sliced
1 to 2 cloves garlic, crushed
¹/₂ cup olive or vegetable oil
2 broiler-fryer chickens, each
  cut into 4 or 8 pieces
1 large can peeled tomatoes
1 can tomato sauce
1 bay leaf
1 to 2 tablespoons or more
  chopped parsley

fresh ground black pepper,
  to taste
¹/₂ cup white wine
1 cup pitted black olives
1 cup pimiento-stuffed green
  olives
¹/₂ to 1 pound fresh
  mushrooms, sliced and
  sautéed

Brown onion and garlic lightly in hot oil. Add chicken and brown on all sides. Add all ingredients, except the olives and mushrooms, and simmer gently until chicken is tender (about 45 minutes). Remove chicken and sauce to a large casserole; mix in olives and mushrooms. Place in a 350 degree oven until thoroughly heated. Serve with rice, French bread and a salad.

This dish may be prepared the day before serving. Just add the olives and mushrooms before heating in the casserole.

Adeline Kohn

Savory Stewed Chicken with Never Fail Dumplings

1 (4 to 5 pound) stewing
   chicken
2 sprigs of parsley
3 or 4 celery tops
1 sliced carrot
1 sliced onion
2 teaspoons salt
1/8 teaspoon pepper

Dumplings:
1 1/2 cups sifted flour
2 teaspoons baking powder
3/4 cups chicken or vegetable
   broth

Clean and cut up chicken. Place in a kettle with just enough boiling water to cover and add vegetables and seasonings. Boil 5 minutes. Turn down heat, simmer gently until tender 2 to 3 hours. Add water if necessary.

Sift together flour and baking powder. Stir in broth only until blended. Drop dumplings by spoonfuls onto boiling chicken. Cook 10 minutes with kettle uncovered and 10 minutes more with kettle covered. Success secret: dumplings should rest on chicken and not settle in the liquid. Remove dumplings and serve on platter with chicken and gravy.

Barbara Quinn

Israeli Coffee Chicken

1 large broiler-fryer chicken,
   cut up
3/4 cup coffee
1/3 cup ketchup
3 tablespoons soy sauce

2 tablespoons lemon juice
2 tablespoons wine vinegar
1 tablespoon olive oil
2 tablespoons brown sugar

Mix liquids and sugar and bring to a boil. Reduce heat and simmer 5 to 10 minutes to reduce. Pour over chicken in shallow baking dish and bake at 350 degrees, uncovered, for 1 hour. Baste. Good served cold as well as hot.

Barbara Daily

Honey-Glazed Cornish Hens with Dried Cranberries

1 tablespoon fat removed
   from hens
1 cup chopped onions
1/4 cup chopped parsley
1 cup dried cranberries
1 1/2 teaspoons cinnamon
1/8 teaspoon ground cloves

1 teaspoon black pepper
1/2 teaspoon salt
4 Cornish hens (about 1
   pound each)
1 cup honey
parsley for garnish

In a fry pan melt fat over medium heat. Remove solid pieces from pan. Sauté onions and parsley for 2 to 3 minutes or until onion is soft and transparent. Stir in dried cranberries and spices. Season hens inside and out with mixture. Place hens on rack in roasting pan. Roast at 350 degrees for 35 to 40 minutes.

Carefully pour enough water in roasting pan to cover the bottom. Spread honey over hens to coat. Return to oven; roast 15 to 20 minutes or until hens are tender and golden brown. Remove hens to heated serving platter and keep warm. Thicken pan juices if necessary and correct seasonings to taste. Generously spoon sauce over hens. Garnish with parsley if desired.

Serves 4.

Barbara Taylor

Easy and Delicious Chicken in Sherry

1 broiler-fryer chicken, cut up
garlic, to taste
salt, to taste
pepper, to taste
paprika, to taste

parsley, chopped, to taste
3 to 4 onions
1 pound fresh mushrooms
1 teaspoon rosemary
1/2 cup sherry

Sauté chicken parts in melted margarine that has been well seasoned with loads of garlic, salt, pepper, paprika and chopped parsley. Place in a deep baking dish and put into oven for about 1 hour at 350 degrees. Sauté onions and mushrooms, more pressed garlic, salt, and pepper in margarine. When the mixture is yellow, add rosemary and sherry. Pour this mixture over the chicken. Bake for another hour or until it is nicely browned; turn or baste as needed.

Maxine Suval

Oven-Fried Chicken

1 chicken, cut up	salt and pepper
2 eggs, beaten	crushed corn flakes

Season eggs with salt and pepper and dip chicken parts in egg and then corn flakes. Place on a greased baking sheet and dot with butter. Bake in a 375 degree oven for ½ hour. Turn chicken pieces over and bake another ½ hour until crisp.

Serves 4.

Norma Robinson

Turkey Ratatouille

1 pound turkey cutlets, cut into 1 inch pieces	1 cup sliced zucchini
2 cups diced eggplant	½ cup diced red bell pepper
½ cup thinly sliced onion, separated into rings	½ coarsely shredded carrot
	1 teaspoon basil
1 to 2 large cloves garlic, minced	1 teaspoon parsley
	salt and pepper, to taste
2 cups diced unpeeled plum tomatoes	¼ cup tomato paste
	1 (8 ounce) can tomato sauce

Combine first four ingredients in a 3 quart casserole; cover with heavy-duty plastic wrap and vent. Microwave at high 4 to 6 minutes, stirring after 3 minutes. Add tomato and next 7 ingredients, and toss gently. Microwave at high 6 to 8 minutes or until turkey is done and zucchini is crisp-tender, stirring after 4 minutes. Stir in tomato paste and tomato sauce. Microwave, uncovered, at high 3 minutes. Stir well. Serve over brown rice for a one-dish meal. This can be cooked in a conventional oven as well.

What is

TZIMMES was a favorite New Year dish of Eastern Europe from the late medieval period. It is derived from the German Zummus, a compote or spicy vegetable concoction.

Sweet Potato and Carrot Tzimmes

2 to 2½ pounds brisket	⅓ cup brown sugar
2 pounds sweet potatoes, peeled and quartered	1 teaspoon cinnamon
	salt and pepper, to taste
2 pounds carrots, coarsely grated	1 cup water

Brown the brisket. Place sweet potatoes in the bottom of a crock pot. Cover with grated carrots. Sprinkle brown sugar and cinnamon over the vegetables. Place brisket on top. Season with salt and pepper. Cover crock pot and cook on low setting for 8 to 10 hours.

Carol Gross

Polynesian Brisket

1 fresh brisket
1 (12 ounce) can unsweetened
   pineapple juice

3 tablespoons soy sauce
1 package dry onion soup mix
3 tablespoons brown sugar

Brown both sides of the brisket under the broiler. Mix the next four ingredients together. Pour mixture over meat; cover tightly and roast at 350 degrees approximately 2½ hours. Test with fork. Just before completely tender, slice. Return slices to marinade and return to oven to finish cooking. Flavor is enhanced by leaving in marinade overnight in refrigerator.

Anita Silver

Beef Brisket

4 pounds beef brisket
1 tablespoon oil
2 cups grapefruit juice
1 (6 ounce) can tomato paste
2 medium onions, sliced
1 clove garlic

2 teaspoons salt
¼ teaspoon Tabasco sauce
3 carrots, sliced
3 ribs celery, sliced
¼ cup brown sugar

Brown meat in oil on top of stove. Combine juice and tomato paste; pour over meat. Add onions, garlic, salt, Tabasco sauce, carrots and celery. Roast, covered, at 350 degrees for 2½ hours.

Ginny Rosenberg

Mickey's Brisket

3 to 4 pounds beef brisket   **3 onions**
Kitchen Bouquet   **salt and pepper, to taste**

Day before serving: Place brisket in large roasting pan. Sprinkle Kitchen Bouquet on each side and massage into meat. Salt and pepper each side of brisket. Slice onions and completely cover meat with onions. Cover brisket ½ way with water. Bake covered at 300 degrees for 3 hours. Cool and refrigerate for at least 8 hours.

Day of serving: Remove fat; slice and place back in pan and cook covered at 350 degrees for 1 hour.

My Grandmother always made the best brisket in the family. Whenever I make brisket and take it to a Potluck, I never have any leftovers. One of the things that made family holidays special was knowing that we would be dining on Mickey's Brisket.

Stuart Pressman

Holiday Brisket

5 pound brisket   **½ cup wine or water**
1 cup dark brown sugar   **1 package dry onion soup**
½ cup cider vinegar

Mix above ingredients together. Pour over brisket. Cover tightly with foil. Bake at 350 degrees for 3 hours. (Check pan periodically to make sure there's enough liquid. Add more water or wine as necessary). You may slice brisket after 3 hours and return it to pan for 1 more hour.

Ann Packer

What is...

CHOLENT *is a slow cooking stew of beans, vegetables, potatoes and a small amount of meat served on the Sabbath afternoon. Cooking began, often in a communal oven, on Friday before the beginning of the Sabbath since no work of any kind was allowed on the Sabbath.*

Cholent with Barley

¹/₂ cup dry lima beans
¹/₂ cup barley
2 tablespoons chicken fat
   or oil
1 onion, chopped

3 garlic cloves, minced
2 pounds beef chuck
salt, pepper and paprika,
   to taste
3 cups or more boiling water

Wash beans well, combine with barley and place in crock pot. In a frying pan, heat fat. Add onion, garlic and beef and cook until browned. Season well with salt, pepper and paprika. Combine onion and garlic with beans in crock pot. Cut beef into 1¹/₂ inch cubes and place on top. Pour on enough boiling water to cover bean mixture. Cover crock pot and cook on low setting overnight. May be cooked in a conventional oven at low setting for appropriate time.

Carol Gross

California Cholent

1½ cups dry black beans
3 to 4 tablespoons olive oil
1 large onion, chopped
5 cloves garlic, minced
1 jalapeño pepper, seeded
   and chopped
3 carrots, sliced in ¼ inch
   slices
1 medium potato, cubed
1½ cups cooked barley

1 (15 ounce) can tomato sauce
   or pureed tomatoes
3½ cups chicken stock
½ cup chopped parsley
1 tablespoon paprika
2 tablespoons flour
4 to 6 pieces of chicken
½ cup white wine
1 tablespoon capers
salt and pepper, to taste

Sort, then soak black beans overnight and cook according to package directions. Heat oil in large and deep pan. Add onion, garlic, jalapeno, carrots and potatoes. Cook until onions and pepper become soft. Add barley, tomatoes, chicken stock, parsley, paprika and flour. Place chicken parts on top of vegetable mixture. Do not crowd chicken parts. Cover pan and simmer for about one hour or cook in a 325 degree oven until done. Stir frequently and add additional broth as necessary. Fifteen minutes before the dish is done, stir in black beans. Stir wine, capers, salt and pepper about 10 minutes before done. Serve with brown rice and salad. This can be cooked traditionally overnight in a very slow oven.

Serves 4 to 6.

Cholent

2 to 4 tablespoons oil
1 large onion, chopped
2 pounds stew meat
5 pounds potatoes, peeled
½ pound beans

½ pound barley
salt and pepper
garlic powder
red pepper (optional)

In a large skillet brown the chopped onions. Add the meat and lightly brown. In a large pot (a turkey roaster is great) combine all the ingredients. Cover with boiling water and bake at 350 degrees for the first hour. Reduce the temperature to 200 degrees and leave for 8 to 10 hours. You can't over cook cholent. The longer you cook it the better. It is advised though to check every 3 to 4 hours and add more boiling water when necessary and to correct seasonings.

Tamar Neta

Creole Stew

3 tablespoons olive oil
1 pound lean beef, cut in 1
   inch cubes
1 onion, coarsely chopped
1 red pepper, seeded and
   coarsely chopped
2 jalapeno peppers, seeded
   and finely chopped
4 cloves garlic, minced
2 tomatoes, seeded and
   chopped
parsley, bay leaf, thyme and
   oregano, to taste

salt and pepper to taste
4 to 5 cups beef stock
1 medium sweet potato, cubed
1 medium white potato, cubed
1 cup pre-soaked small white
   beans
2 tart apples, diced
2 zucchini, cut in 1 inch slices
2 ears of corn, cut in 2 inch
   slices
12 dried apricots

Heat oil in heavy flame proof casserole and brown meat well. Add onion, pepper, jalapenos, garlic, and tomatoes and cook until onion is soft. Add herbs, salt and pepper, stock and beans. Cover, reduce heat and simmer about one hour. Add potatoes and continue to cook until tender. During cooking add more stock if necessary. Add remaining ingredients and cook 5 minutes or until done. This is a great dish because it uses so very little meat and yet tastes hearty.

Serves 6.

Joyce Kurtz

Meat Balls and Cabbage

1¹/₂ pounds ground beef
1 medium head cabbage
1 medium onion, finely
   chopped
salt and pepper

1 bottle chili sauce
1 can cranberries
1 tablespoon brown sugar
10 ounces water

Mix meat, spices and onion and form meat balls. Slice cabbage and cover the bottom of a casserole with it. Add layer of meatballs and top with remaining cabbage.

In separate bowl mix chili sauce, cranberries, brown sugar and water (1 chili sauce bottle full will do). Pour sauce over casserole and cover. Bake at 350 degrees for 2 hours, uncover and bake another hour. Serve over rice.

Betty Unger

Sweet and Sour Tongue

1 fresh tongue
4 bay leaves
6 peppercorns
1 onion
2 or 3 carrots
$1/4$ teaspoon salt
Sauce:
1 large onion
1 tablespoon chicken fat or
  oil

1 tablespoon flour
$1/2$ teaspoon salt
1 stick cinnamon or a good
  dash of ground cinnamon
$1/4$ cup chopped almonds
$1/4$ cup seedless raisins
$1/4$ cup brown sugar
1 tablespoon maple syrup
juice of 1 large lemon

Boil tongue with bay leaves, peppercorns, onion, carrots and salt until soft. Skim when necessary as with soup. Skin, slice and arrange in a casserole dish. Reserve at least $3^{1}/_{2}$ cups of stock.

Sauce: Sauté diced onion in oil until golden brown. Sprinkle with flour. Add 3 cups of strained hot liquid, slowly, while stirring. Then add all the other ingredients and simmer for 10 minutes. Taste and add salt, if necessary. Pour over the tongue. (This can be left in the refrigerator for several days until needed.)

When required, put in a slow oven (about 300 degrees) without lid for $1^{1}/_{2}$ hours, basting occasionally. Add an occasional tablespoon of extra stock, if necessary.

Lorraine Gerstl

JoAnne's Stuffed Cabbage

3 onions, sliced
1/2 cup washed raw rice
1 can tomato soup
1 can water
1/2 bottle chili sauce
juice of 2 lemons
1/2 cup brown sugar

2 pounds ground beef
2 grated onions
1 cup water
2 teaspoons salt
2 eggs
pepper
2 heads of cabbage

In a large roaster put the sliced onions, 1/4 cup rice, soup, 1 soup can water, chili sauce, lemon juice and brown sugar.

Mix together in a bowl the meat, grated onions, 1 cup of water, 1/4 cup rice, salt and pepper.

Cut core from 2 heads of cabbage and put cabbage in boiling water. Separate leaves and soften. Put 1 tablespoon meat in each cabbage leaf and roll. Put cabbage rolls in roaster. Put in 325 degree oven for 3 to 4 hours.

JoAnne Rockower

Unstuffed Cabbage

1 large onion, sliced
1 large can whole berry
   cranberry sauce
1 pound ground beef
3 cloves garlic, minced
1 egg

1 cabbage, quartered
1 medium jar spaghetti sauce
1 cup chopped onion
1/2 cup raw rice
salt and pepper, to taste

Line bottom of large pot with sliced onion. Combine ground beef, chopped onion, garlic, rice, egg, salt and pepper. Divide meat mixture in half, then in half again. Divide each quarter into thirds, giving you 12 meat balls. Cut each quarter of cabbage into thirds, giving you 12 cabbage wedges. Place meat balls and cabbage on top of sliced onions and cover with mixture of spaghetti sauce and cranberry sauce. Cover. Bring slowly to a boil, lower to simmer and simmer 2 hours. Or put into 350 degree oven, bring to a boil, and cook 2 hours longer at 300 degrees. This recipe has all the flavor and none of the work of cabbage rolls.

Makes 12 appetizer or 4 to 6 main course servings.

Bonni Weinstein

Cabbage Rolls

1 large head of cabbage
1 pound ground beef
½ cup cooked rice
½ large onion, grated
1 egg
½ teaspoon pepper
1 (6 ounce) can tomato paste

1 (8 ounce) can tomato sauce
1 cup water
¼ teaspoon sage
1 bay leaf
¼ cup packed brown sugar
2 or 3 tablespoons lemon juice
(or vinegar)

Remove core from cabbage and cover cabbage with boiling water; let stand for 15 minutes. Mix ground beef and the next 5 ingredients. Stir in 2 tablespoons tomato paste. Drain cabbage and separate the leaves carefully. Place a heaping tablespoon of meat mixture (oval shaped) on each leaf. Tuck in the sides and carefully roll up cabbage leaves. You may have to use toothpicks to hold them together.

Consider every cabbage leaf a challenge to roll — those leaves that fail the test should be shredded and placed on the bottom of the pan. Gently place cabbage rolls on shredded cabbage. Combine remaining tomato paste and next 4 ingredients; pour over cabbage rolls. Cover and simmer over low heat, or place in 375 degree oven for 1 hour, then uncover pan, baste and put in oven again for 20 to 30 minutes to brown slightly. If any are left, they taste even better reheated.

Also known as Holiskes, Praakes, Galuptzi, or when raisins are added to sauce, Sarma.

Zane Speiser

Stuffed Breast of Veal

1 breast of veal with pocket
   cut
3 baking potatoes, cooked
   and coarsely mashed
1 pound fresh spinach,
   chopped
2 large carrots, finely diced
1 onion, chopped
2 whole eggs, beaten, or
   equivalent egg substitute
salt, white pepper and
   paprika

2 chopped garlic cloves
$3/4$ tablespoon olive oil
Braising ingredients:
1 quart veal or brown stock
   (canned beef broth can be
   used)
2 onions, coarsely chopped
3 or 4 stalks of celery,
   chopped
1 large onion, chopped

Combine all stuffing ingredients to taste. Salt and pepper the inside of the cavity and fill, loosely. Stitch securely with butcher twine. Preheat olive oil in a large skillet until almost smoking. Brown roast on all sides, starting with fatty side. Remove from pan when brown and pour off oil. Pour braising liquid and vegetables over veal to cover $3/4$ of it. Cover pan securely. Place in a 375 degree oven for approximately $1^1/2$ to 2 hours. Insert meat thermometer in the center of stuffing. When thermometer reads 165 to 170 degrees, remove roast from juice. Remove vegetables from liquid and purée with liquid. Adjust seasonings. Slice, pour gravy over meat and serve.

Neal Rosenthal

My brother, the chef, took our mother's traditional Breast of Veal recipe and expanded on it. She now calls him from Florida when she cooks this.

Linda Kaiser

Sweet and Sour Leg of Lamb

4 to 5 pounds leg of lamb
4 cloves garlic, slivered
1/2 cup raisins, preferably
   sultanas
1 teaspoon thyme
1 teaspoon marjoram
1 slice whole wheat bread,
   thick, crumbled
2 large onions, quartered
1/2 cup stock

Glaze:
2 tablespoons apricot
   preserves, or peach jelly
   or jam
1 tablespoon lemon juice
2 tablespoons brown sugar
2 tablespoons Worcestershire
   sauce
2 tablespoons tomato sauce

Make several incisions in the leg and fill with crumb mixture. Fry 2 quartered onions in oil. Add meat and brown on all sides. Season with salt and pepper. Add 1/2 cup stock. Cover tightly and place in 350 degree oven for 2 1/2 hours. Meanwhile, make glaze by heating glaze mixture. Uncover meat and pour over half the glaze. Continue cooking. Fifteen minutes later, remove and place on serving platter. Make gravy by adding 1 cup stock to pan drippings.

Lorraine Gerstl

Piquant Lamb

1 small leg of lamb
2 tablespoons margarine
1 large onion, sliced
1 teaspoon salt
1/2 teaspoon pepper
1 tablespoon flour
1 cup dry white wine

1 1/4 cups stock
4 chopped anchovy fillets
   (optional)
1 tablespoon parsley
1 clove garlic, chopped
1/2 teaspoon grated lemon
   rind

Place meat, margarine and onion in a heavy sauce pan; add salt and pepper. Brown meat slowly, but thoroughly, turning often to prevent burning. When brown, sprinkle with flour, and cook slowly until wine evaporates. Add stock; cover saucepan and cook slowly for 1 1/2 hours or until meat is tender. Add anchovies (optional), parsley, garlic and lemon rind, stirring into gravy. Cook 1 minute, turning meat once.

Serves 6.

Lorraine Gerstl

Gefilte Fish Loaf

3 medium whole carrots
2 pounds whitefish fillet
2 medium onions, chopped
1 carrot, grated
scant ½ cup matzo meal
1 teaspoon vegetable oil
1 whole egg

2 egg whites
1 teaspoon sugar
dash of salt
white pepper, to taste
½ teaspoon nutmeg
½ cup cold water

Grind or process fish and onion. Combine with grated carrot, matzo meal, oil, sugar, salt, pepper, eggs, and cold water. Mix well. Place half of mixture in a non-stick or lightly greased 9x5x3 inch loaf pan. Arrange the three whole carrots lengthwise on top of this mixture and top with the remaining half of the mixture. Bake at 350 degrees for 1 hour and cool in the pan. Turn out and refrigerate, covered. Slice and serve with horseradish. (This is fairly low in fat and cholesterol. To make fat and cholesterol free, omit the teaspoon of oil and use 4 egg whites or 4 ounces of egg substitute.)

Makes 6 to 8 servings.

Bonni Weinstein

A Chanukah recipe

Start with a handful of uplifting stories of Jewish courage and history and a pinch of jazz and a pitzel of klezmer. Drizzle in a dash of dreidel. Pepper with Chanukah songs until everyone sings. Blend all ingredients well and let set for an hour. Serves the entire family and friends.

Anna Shelkowsky

Microwave Fish Filets

1 pound fish filets	scallions
1/4 cup vermouth	mushrooms
fresh rosemary and oregano	salt and pepper

Pour vermouth in bottom of a 9x13 inch glass baking pan. Add chopped scallions and sliced mushrooms. Place fish in pan with thicker pieces around the outside and thinner pieces toward the middle of the dish. Season and cover with plastic film and pierce with a knife. Microwave on high for 6 to 7 minutes, turning midway. Let stand 2 to 3 minutes and serve.

Linda Kaiser

Grilled Salmon with Gazpacho Salsa

1 medium cucumber, peeled, seeded, 1/4 inch dice	3 tablespoons red wine vinegar
1 red pepper, 1/4 inch dice	1 tablespoon Worcestershire sauce
1 medium red onion, 1/4 inch dice	1 teaspoon hot pepper sauce
2 large beefsteak tomatoes, seeded, 1/4 inch dice	1/4 cup olive oil
	6 salmon steaks

In medium bowl, place all but salmon. Mix. Place 1/3 in food processor and purée until smooth. Stir into remaining vegetables. Cover. Set aside at room temperature for 1 hour. Grill salmon steaks. Divide salsa over hot fish and serve at once.

Freda Golding

Spinach Zucchini Lasagna

1 (8 ounce) package lasagna
noodles
12 ounces grated mozzarella
cheese
16 ounces ricotta cheese
1 (10 ounce) package frozen
chopped spinach
1/4 cup grated Parmesan
cheese
3 medium zucchini squash,
thinly sliced
1/4 pound mushrooms, sliced
1 red or green bell pepper,
chopped

1 onion, finely chopped
2 cloves garlic, minced
3 tablespoons oil
1 (8 ounce) can tomato sauce
1 (28 ounce) can tomatoes,
chopped
1/2 cup red wine
1/2 teaspoon salt
1/2 teaspoon pepper
1 teaspoon oregano and basil
1/4 teaspoon thyme
1 teaspoon hot sauce
or 1/8 teaspoon cayenne
pepper

To prepare sauce: Sauté zucchini, mushrooms, bell pepper, onions and garlic in oil in a large frying pan until vegetables are soft and slightly browned. Add wine, seasonings and tomato products. Simmer over low heat, uncovered, about 20 to 30 minutes.

While sauce is cooking, prepare the other ingredients. Cook noodles according to package directions. Drain and rinse in cold water. Set aside. Cook spinach according to package directions. Put spinach in a colander and using a wooden spoon press out all liquid. Combine spinach with ricotta cheese.

Put a small amount of sauce in a 9x13 inch baking dish. Then alternately layer noodles, ricotta-spinach mixture, sauce and mozzarella cheese. Repeat two more times ending with sauce, then mozzarella. Sprinkle Parmesan cheese over last layer. Bake at 350 degrees uncovered for 45 minutes.

Serves 8 to 10.

Barbara Mitchell

The history of the Sephardic Jews, the Jews from the Mediterranean, may not be as well known as that of the Ashkenazi Jews, those from Europe. The food is considerably different. Matzo balls, gefilte fish and bagels are not part of our cuisine. Ours is of a more Mediterranean flavor.

At the time of the Spanish Inquisition in 1492, when Jews were required to convert to Christianity or were ordered to leave Spain, they fled to all parts of Europe. The Ottomans welcomed them, knowing that they were educated and had contributed greatly to the Spanish Empire. They were teachers, doctors, poets, bankers and some had served as trusted advisors to the King and Queen of Spain.

After settlement in Rhodes, my family retained their Old Spanish language, Ladino. Under Turkish, Greek and Italian rule, the Jews of Rhodes combined their Spanish food and the local food into what it is today.

Esther Stern

Pink Spanish Rice

1 cup long grain rice	2 cups water or chicken broth
1 teaspoon salt	2 tablespoons tomato sauce
1 teaspoon oil	

Bring to boil and add rice. Let it come to a boil again, stir rice, cover, then bake at 350 degrees for 15 to 20 minutes until done and water evaporates. Remove from oven and fluff up with a fork.

Esther Stern

Yaprakis (Stuffed Grape Leaves)

1 small jar grape leaves,
    rinsed, drained and stems
    removed
1 cup white beans
Filling:
1 pound lean ground beef
1/4 cup rice
1 teaspoon salt
pepper to taste

1 tablespoon oil
1/4 cup chopped parsley
2 tablespoons tomato sauce
Sauce:
2 teaspoons oil
1/4 cup tomato sauce
2 cups water
juice of 1 lemon to add after
    yaprakis are tender

Boil beans 30 minutes and drain. Mix filling ingredients together. On each grape leaf, vein side up, place about a heaping teaspoon of filling and roll up in cigar shape, tucking in sides. In a casserole, place beans and rolls in layers, beginning and ending with beans. Make sure the rolls are placed close together. Pour sauce over all. Make sure sauce covers all. A few grape leaves may be added on top to cover. Cover pan and cook in oven at 350 degrees for 2 to 3 hours or until tender, adding lemon juice towards end of cooking. These are better reheated the next day. We serve these with our Pink Spanish Rice.

Esther Stern

Keftes

1 1/2 pounds lamb, ground
1 1/2 teaspoons dried mint
    leaves
1 cup bread crumbs, soft
1 1/2 tablespoons ketchup
2 eggs

1 medium onion, finely
    chopped
1/2 teaspoon salt
1/8 teaspoon pepper
1/2 teaspoon cinnamon
1/8 teaspoon allspice

Combine all. Make 15 to 18 patties in an oblong shape. Bake at 350 degrees uncovered for 15 minutes, turn and bake an additional 15 minutes. Serve at room temperature with lots of lemon wedges as an appetizer or serve hot with rice or bulgar pilaf.

Serves 6.

Ethel Alvy

Hungarian Hortobágyi Palacsinta

Batter:
1½ cups flour
2 cups soda water or milk
3 eggs
pinch of salt

Filling:
2 pounds mushrooms
1 red bell pepper
1 large onion (red is favorite)
1 cup shredded Swiss cheese
Hungarian red paprika

Batter: Mix flour, eggs, soda water or milk and salt together. On gentle heat in a medium size skillet fry the pancakes (palacsinta), in very little oil, on both sides (one ladle of batter for each palacsinta). Stack them on a large plate.

Filling: Sauté finely chopped onion in a little oil, add a teaspoon of Hungarian red paprika and the sliced mushrooms and red bell pepper. Season to your taste and stir fry for 2 minutes.

Place 2 palacsintas in a casserole dish and top it with ⅓ of filling; continue layering palacsintas and filling. Cover top palacsintas with shredded cheese and sprinkle with Hungarian red paprika. Bake uncovered in moderate oven for 30 to 40 minutes. Serve it with yogurt. Jo etvágyat! (Good appetite!).

Ilona Milch

This recipe is a favorite on the Great Plains area of Hungary. It is usually made with meat and wine sauce, but I prefer vegetable filling, especially mushroom. Since we live in this "superb fresh mushroom" growing area, I think it is appropriate to bake this dish year round.

Ilona Milch

Spicy Autumn Veggie Stew

3 tablespoons oil (corn, light olive, or light sesame)

1 to 2 onions, peeled and diced

1 to 2 chilis, fresh or dried to suit your taste (serrano or ancho are best)

2 to 3 garlic cloves, peeled and finely chopped or pressed

1 tablespoon paprika, hot or sweet

1 teaspoon cumin seeds or powder

1 teaspoon oregano leaves or powder

1 teaspoon cinnamon or piece cinnamon stick

1/4 teaspoon cloves or 3 whole cloves

1/2 teaspoon salt

3 cups pumpkin or squash (acorn, hubbard, winter) or sweet potatoes, or yams, peeled and cut into cubes

1 pound tomatoes, fresh or canned

2 cups broth, canned or fresh vegetable or chicken (also can use tomato or carrot juice)

2 cups cooked beans, pinto, great northern, cannelini or kidney; canned and drained or cooked from dried (allow 1 hour to soak, 1 hour to cook; 1 cup beans to 4 cups water)

1 cup corn, sliced off fresh ears or frozen kernels

cilantro or parsley (optional for garnish)

Sauté onions until soft in oil in large sauté pan or Dutch oven. Add chilis, garlic, paprika, cumin, oregano, cinnamon and cloves. Stir over low heat for one minute. Add salt, uncooked squash and stir well, add tomatoes and broth. Cover and cook 1/2 hour over low heat, stirring occasionally. Add cooked beans and corn and continue cooking until squash or pumpkin is tender. Canned beans will fall apart if added before the last 15 minutes cooking time.

Maria Gitin Cozzini

Esau's Stew

⅓ cup chopped onions
½ cup chopped celery
½ cup chopped carrots
5 tablespoons butter or
    olive oil
5 cups water or stock

1 cup dried lentils
½ cup barley
⅛ teaspoon rosemary
2 teaspoons cumin
salt, to taste

In a large pot, sauté the onions, celery and carrots in the butter or oil. Add water or stock, lentils, celery and seasonings. Bring to a boil, turn down the heat and cook until barley and lentil are tender, about 1 hour.

Serves 6 to 8.

Vegetarian Stew with Couscous

3 tablespoons olive oil
1 large eggplant, cut in
    ½ inch cubes
1 pound zucchini, cut in
    ½ inch cubes
2 (14½ ounce) cans seasoned
    for pasta, cut up tomatoes,
    undrained
6 scallions, cut in ½ inch
    pieces

1 tablespoon red wine
    vinegar
1 teaspoon dried thyme
salt to taste
½ teaspoon pepper
1 (19 ounce) can chick peas or
    cook up dried chick peas
4 ounces feta cheese, diced
1 cup dry couscous, prepared
    according to package
    directions

Heat 2 tablespoons oil in a Dutch oven over medium high heat. Add eggplant and cook 4 minutes, stirring often, until lightly browned. Add zucchini and remaining oil. Cook 3 minutes, stirring once or twice. Add 1 can tomatoes, scallions, vinegar, and seasonings. Cook 5 minutes, stirring often or until vegetables are tender and most liquid has evaporated. Add remaining can of tomatoes and chick peas. Cook until hot. Remove from heat, stir in feta and serve over hot couscous.

Serves 4.

Joyce Kurtz

Jewish Spaghetti

8 ounces spaghetti, boiled
  and drained
1 can tomato soup
1 small can tomato sauce
1 small onion, peeled and
  coarsely chopped

1 green pepper, cored and
  chopped
1/2 pound mushrooms, sliced
grated Parmesan cheese

Brown the onion and green pepper in a little oil or butter, adding the mushrooms for a few minutes at the end. Mix all ingredients together in a casserole, sprinkle cheese over the top and bake in a 375 degree oven until brown.

This is a great vegetarian dish and a favorite of my mother, Yetta Lieberman. The family loved it. It was born during the Great Depression and is economical, easy to make, and delicious.

Adeline Kohn

Roasted Red Pepper Sauce

8 unpeeled cloves garlic
3 large red peppers, roasted,
  peeled and cored
1/2 cup water
1/4 cup unblanched almonds
1/4 cup fine dry bread crumbs

2 tablespoons red wine
  vinegar
2 tablespoons olive oil
1/2 teaspoon salt
2 pounds pasta cooked
2 tablespoons minced parsley

Roast foil wrapped garlic in 400 degree oven for 20 minutes. Cool, squeeze out of skins. Process garlic, peppers, water, almonds, bread crumbs, vinegar, oil and salt until pureed. Heat sauce and pour over hot pasta, toss with parsley and fresh ground Parmesan cheese. Serve baby greens salad and raspberry vinaigrette topped with a sprinkling of pecan pralines.

Cathleen Connell

Pasta Sauce

vegetable oil pan spray
1 pound fresh button
   mushrooms, thinly sliced
2 pounds onions, coarsely
   chopped by hand (not food
   processor)
4 cloves garlic, finely chopped
1 (6 pound, 8 ounce) can
   whole peeled tomatoes,
   pureed in food processor
   (or equivalent amount of
   canned crushed tomatoes)
3 (12 ounce) cans tomato
   paste
1½ teaspoons freshly ground
   black pepper
1½ teaspoons whole dried
   fennel seed, ground in
   spice grinder
5 small whole dried bay
   leaves
1 tablespoon dried oregano
   leaves
1 tablespoon dried basil
   leaves
1 teaspoon dried hot red
   pepper flakes

Spray a 12 inch skillet with pan spray. Add mushrooms and stir to coat. "Sweat" the mushrooms, covered, until they are soft and there is still some of their natural liquid in the pan. Set aside.

Spray an 8 quart kettle with pan spray. Stir in the chopped onions and garlic and sauté, covered, very slowly over low to medium heat. Use a spatula frequently to scrape the browned layer off the bottom of the kettle back into the onions. Cook until the mixture is deep amber in color, greatly reduced in bulk, and very sweet.

To the onion-garlic mixture in the kettle, add the cooked mushrooms, tomato puree, tomato paste, and all seasonings. Stir, cover and bring gradually to a boil over medium heat to prevent scorching; then reduce heat immediately to the lowest setting that will maintain a slow simmer. Simmer covered for 2 hours, stirring occasionally and scraping the sweet browned layer at the bottom of the kettle back into the sauce.

Karen Wiskoff

Passover

Passover

Passover, the eight day spring festival, celebrates the deliverance of our ancestors from slavery in Egypt and our becoming a People. The first night of Passover is marked by a Seder, a home-centered ritual retelling of the Exodus story while enjoying a special meal complete with ritual foods. Children play an important part in the Seder asking questions and learning the meaning and story of the symbolic foods. Passover is a combination of two ancient agricultural celebrations: a family celebration called the Pesach meal, dating back to desert days, from which our Seder developed and the week-long Feast of the Unleavened Bread which developed later as the Hebrews became farmers. It is a time to open our homes to our friends and members of the community.

We are told, that during the Exodus, Jews fled in great haste and didn't have time to let their dough rise. Matzo, the unleavened bread reminds us of this flight and struggle. No leavened foods, legumes, or rice are served during the week. Products made from matzo using its various forms, as flour, meal, crumbed and crackers replace any other grain. Not only are these foods not served but they are removed from the house. In Sephardic homes the same traditions are observed but different foods are prepared, reflecting their Mediterranean background.

Traditionally, there is a Seder on each of the first two nights. On the second night a Seder might be held at the synagogue to allow the community to observe together and to insure all who wish to attend a Seder have the opportunity to do so. Feminist Seders are now becoming more common, giving women a chance to gather and retell their unique role in the deliverance.

What is...

CHAROSET is a combination of nuts, dried or fresh fruits, spices and sweet wine. Served on Passover with matzos and horseradish. It symbolizes the mortar used by the Hebrew slaves in Egypt.

Charoset

1 apple, pared
1/2 cup crushed walnuts
1/2 teaspoon cinnamon

1 teaspoon honey or sugar
2 tablespoons red wine

Coarsely grate apple. Mix with remaining ingredients until mixture is very smooth.

Judy Reibel

Charoset

2 pounds dates
1 pound chopped walnuts,
   almonds or pecans

Passover grape wine

Boil dates in water to barely cover until tender and water is evaporated. Mix dates and nuts. Add wine to moisten. Chill.

Esther Stern

Chrain

1/2 pound horseradish root,
   peeled and grated
1 beet, peeled and grated
1/2 cup cider vinegar

1/4 cup water
1/4 cup sugar
1/2 teaspoon salt

Combine ingredients and taste for seasoning. Place in jar. Keep tightly closed.

Susan Gorelick

What is...

Matzos or unleavened bread dates back to the Exodus from Egypt. Of more recent history, Old World matzos were considerably different from those we buy in supermarkets today. Made and shaped entirely by hand in communal bakeries, those matzos were either round or oval and much thicker than the commercial ones we now eat. The rich customers might tip the baker to secure thinner matzos. Square matzos, later called the American style, were first made by machine in Austria in 1857. As late as 1912 they were still not manufactured in London and had to be imported from the continent. The women of Italy took pride in shaping a perfect oval shape matzo adding eyelets and festoons. Finely detailed, they could be made to look like pieces of art.

Matzo Balls

½ cup matzo meal, heaping
3 eggs
1 teaspoon salt
¼ teaspoon pepper
1 teaspoon dried parsley
¼ teaspoon dried thyme

1 to 2 tablespoons chicken fat or oil
1 small onion, finely chopped
1 tablespoon water or chicken broth

Beat together eggs and matzo meal. Add seasonings. Sauté onions in fat until golden. Cool onions then add to mixture. Add broth or water. Cover and refrigerate 1 to 3 hours. Roll into 16 to 18 balls about the size of small walnuts (use a teaspoon to scoop up batter and dust hands with extra matzo meal to combat stickiness). Drop balls into boiling water and cook for 10 minutes. Then transfer to hot broth for another 10 minutes before serving. This recipe can easily be doubled for a larger family gathering.

Serves 6.

Diana Rosenthal

No-Fat Matzo Balls

1 cup egg substitute	1 cup matzo meal
(equivalent to 4 eggs)	5 tablespoons soda water
1½ teaspoons salt	

Mix all and chill for 1 hour. To shape, roll a small ball with cold water, dampen palms of hands and shape mixture into walnut-sized balls. Bring a large pot of salted water to rolling boil, reduce to simmer and add matzo balls. Simmer 25 to 30 minutes.

Makes 12 large balls.

Bonni Weinstein

Leaning Tower of Matzos

10 slices matzo	½ cup chopped walnuts or
1 tablespoon butter	pecans
2 tablespoons brandy, orange	10 ounces semi-sweet
liqueur or orange juice	chocolate bits
1 cup white wine,	¾ cup orange marmalade
dry or sweet	shredded peel of 1 orange

Melt butter and chocolate bits, add marmalade. Stir in eggs and brandy or juice. Pour wine in wide shallow bowl or rimmed plate. Use wax paper to line a serving plate big enough to hold a whole matzo. Dip each matzo slice quickly on both sides in wine, lay on wax paper and spread with chocolate mixture. Stack slices evenly on top each other and spread remaining mixture on top and sides of stack. Decorate with nuts sprinkled evenly over top and orange peel on top. Chill overnight to give matzos time to soften.

Carefully peel off waxed paper and transfer to serving dish. People laugh when they hear and see this, but it beats dry sponge cake any day and just wait until they taste it! You can make a delicious low fat no sugar version by deleting the butter, substituting 8 ounces of low fat no sugar hot fudge sauce for the chocolate, using no sugar marmalade and leaving out the nuts.

Bonni Weinstein

Matzo Balls

4 eggs
1/2 cup water

3 tablespoons chicken fat
1¹/₆ cups matzo meal

Beat eggs 15 minutes. Add salt and pepper to taste. Gradually add cold water and beat another 5 minutes. Add chicken fat. Mix in matzo meal by hand and refrigerate overnight. Make balls, bring salt water to a boil, and simmer for about 40 minutes, loosely covered.

Judy Reibel

Ode to the Best Matzo Balls

Last year on the morning of the first Seder I received a phone call from a woman in Oregon. She told me she was a cousin of a woman I knew in Miami many years ago and with whom I had lost touch. This Oregon woman had been to a Seder a number of years earlier where her cousin had served my mother's matzo balls and she was compelled to thank me, so somehow she found me here in Carmel.

Isn't it amazing how gratitude travels not only across the country but also through time, back to my mother and probably to hers.

Judy Reibel

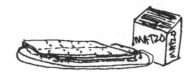

Matzo Balls

3 eggs, separated
³/₄ cup matzo meal
¹/₂ teaspoon salt

chopped dill or parsley
(optional)

Beat egg whites until stiff. Beat egg yolks and salt until thick. Fold in egg whites and then gradually fold in the matzo meal. Chill for one hour. Moisten hands; shape into ¹/₂ inch balls. Cook in boiling salted water about 20 minutes.

Barbara Lipman

What is...

KNEIDLECH is the Yiddish word for dumpling. In the winter, big dumplings were made from potato dough and were often filled with oatmeal, chopped onions, and goose or chicken fat; smaller, more digestible dumplings were made from mashed potatoes that were placed in a bowl of warm milk. Today, kneidlech made from matzo meal are served in chicken soup at Passover and the year round.

Matzo Brie or Matzo Fry

2 matzos
2 eggs

butter or margarine
salt and pepper, to taste

Break the matzos into small pieces. Soak in cold water until soft and drain. Beat the eggs and salt together and pour over the matzos. Fry in butter or margarine until brown on both sides or scramble. If you are making it pancake style, serve with jam, and leave out pepper.

Serves 1.

Rick and Linda Kaiser

When Rick and I got married, we had an argument over how to make Matzo Brie. My mother made it pancake style and his mother made it scrambled. Either way the ingredients are basically the same.

Linda Kaiser

Stupendous Potato Kugel

12 russet potatoes, grated and
  strained
6 eggs
1 cup matzo meal
1 teaspoon baking powder

$1/2$ cup schmaltz, with some
  extra
1 tablespoon salt
$1/4$ teaspoon white pepper
2 medium onions, finely
  chopped

Beat eggs. Mix potatoes, onions, baking powder, pepper, salt, matzo meal and $1/4$ cup of schmaltz, and quickly add to beaten eggs. Put remaining $1/4$ cup of schmaltz in a 9x13 inch glass baking dish and heat in a 350 degree oven until really hot. Then add kugel mixture and dot with a little bit of schmaltz. Bake at 350 degrees for $1 1/2$ hours.

Lorraine Gerstl

Matzo Kugel

6 matzos
2 tablespoons melted
  margarine
6 eggs (or equivalent egg
  substitute)
1 (15 ounce) can unsweetened
  applesauce

½ cup granulated sugar
¼ cup milk (regular, low fat
  or non-fat)
white raisins (or cut up dried
  fruit bits)
cinnamon and sugar

Soak the matzos in warm water. Squeeze out the liquid. Toss with melted margarine. Beat eggs, add applesauce, sugar, milk and raisins. Mix together all ingredients. Spray a 2 quart pan with non-stick vegetable spray. Bake at 375 degrees for 1 hour.

Linda Kaiser

Low-Cholesterol Potato Kugel

2 pounds potatoes, peeled and
  grated
1 small or medium onion,
  grated

4 egg whites
4 tablespoons matzo meal
1 teaspoon salt
dash white pepper

Drain the grated potatoes. Mix well with all the other ingredients. Bake in a greased 8 inch pan at 350 degrees for 35 minutes or until firm.

Linda Kaiser

Mushroom Farfel Kugel

½ pound sliced mushrooms
1 celery stalk, chopped
1 medium onion, chopped
3 tablespoons olive oil

4 cups matzo farfel
1½ teaspoons salt
2 egg whites

Sauté the mushrooms, celery and onion in oil over medium heat until soft (10 to 15 minutes). Cover the matzo farfel with water and soak for a few minutes. Drain well in a colander. Mix the farfel, sautéed vegetables, salt and egg whites. Bake in a well greased (non-stick vegetable spray) 8 inch square baking dish, covered, in 350 degree oven for 30 minutes.

Linda Kaiser

Matzo Farfel Kugel

1 cup boiling water
2 cups farfel
2 eggs, beaten
3/4 cups sugar
1 teaspoon cinnamon

1/2 cup raisins
3 apples, pared and diced
1/2 cup walnuts, chopped
coarsely

Pour boiling water over farfel and soak for 5 minutes, covered; then drain. Mix farfel with all the remaining ingredients. Pour into a greased 9x13 inch pan. Bake uncovered in a 350 degree oven for 45 minutes.

Adeline Kohn

Farfel Stuffing

1 cup farfel
1 egg, beaten
1/2 teaspoon salt
1/2 cup chopped mushrooms

chicken schmaltz
1 small onion
1/4 cup warm water

Mix farfel and warm water. Add salt. Sauté onion in small amount of schmaltz. Add beaten egg. Mix in the mushrooms. Stuff chicken before roasting.

Yields 2 cups stuffing.

Malka Hanna

Farfel

1 1/4 cups egg farfel
4 cups boiling chicken broth
2 onions, peeled and sliced

1/2 pound sliced mushrooms
chicken fat or oil

Fry 2 onions in fat or oil and add the mushrooms. Remove from pan and brown the farfel. Combine the above in a casserole and pour the chicken broth over all. Let stand for 45 minutes. It will begin to thicken. Bake, covered, at 400 degrees for 1 hour and 15 minutes.

Norma Robinson

Matzo Farfel

1 pound matzo farfel	2 cups boiling water
2 eggs, beaten	2 chicken bouillon cubes
2 large onions, chopped	salt, pepper and paprika, to
½ cup oil	taste

Mix matzo farfel with beaten eggs. Put into a shallow baking pan. Bake at 375 degrees for 30 minutes. Sauté onions in oil with salt, pepper and paprika, in a Dutch oven until brown. Add boiling water, to which bouillon cubes have been added. Add cooked farfel and cover. Cook over a low flame for 20 minutes.

Judy Reibel

Passover Quajado de Carne (Meat Casserole)

2 pounds lean ground beef	1 teaspoon salt
2 onions, chopped	pepper to taste
1 tablespoon oil	¼ cup chopped parsley
1 cup farfel, soaked in water	8 eggs, beaten
and squeezed dry	

Brown onions, then meat in oil. Cool. Add salt and pepper, parsley and farfel. Add 2 beaten eggs at a time to mixture until 6 eggs have been used. Pour in greased 9x13 inch pan and spread last 2 eggs over top. Bake 35 minutes or until golden brown in 400 degree oven.

Esther Stern

Passover Burmelos (Farfel Puffs)

2 cups farfel, soaked in water
  and squeezed dry
2 eggs, well beaten
½ teaspoon salt

½ cup Parmesan cheese,
  grated
oil, for deep frying

Mix all together. Drop mixture by tablespoonful into hot oil until golden brown on all sides. Drain on paper towels. They will be round and puffy. Serve hot with strawberry jam.

Esther Stern

Spinaka

1½ boxes matzos
4 packages frozen chopped
  spinach
4 large eggs
1 pound feta cheese

½ pound hard sharp cheese,
  such as asiago or kassari,
  grated
½ cup canola oil

Crumble matzos into small pieces into a bowl and moisten with water until matzos begin to stick together. Mix in defrosted spinach, beaten eggs, feta cheese, oil and all but ¾ cup of cheese.

Lightly oil 2 (10x18 inch) baking sheets completely. Divide mixture covering pans evenly. Sprinkle reserved cheese over tops. Bake until crisp, 35 to 40 minutes at 350 degrees.

Shelly Glaser

Chicken Collachlach (Meatballs)

1½ pounds boneless chicken
  breasts
1 tablespoon matzo meal
4 teaspoons sugar
4 eggs

2 onions
salt, to taste
pepper, to taste
2 carrots

Grind 1 onion and chicken. Add eggs and sugar. Add matzo meal. Moisten hands and form mixture into balls about 1 to 1½ inches in diameter. Bring 2½ quarts water to boil with 1 onion (sliced) and 2 carrots (sliced). Add meatballs. Simmer for 1½ hours. Add sugar or salt to water for last 10 minutes of cooking to adjust to taste.

Shelli Klein

Passover Orange Chicken

1 egg	1 frying chicken, cut up
1/2 cup matzo meal	1 1/3 cups orange juice
water	12 prunes
3/4 teaspoon salt	1 orange, thinly sliced
1/4 teaspoon pepper	

Beat together 1 egg and 1 teaspoon water. Mix matzo meal, salt and pepper together. Dip chicken in egg mixture; roll in matzo meal to coat. Brown chicken pieces on all sides in a little oil. Add orange juice and prunes. Cover and simmer 30 minutes, basting chicken occasionally. Add 1 thinly sliced orange and continue cooking 10 more minutes.

Anita Silver

9 Egg Sponge Cake

9 eggs, separated, at room temperature	1/4 cup lemon juice
2 cups sugar	1/2 teaspoon salt, if desired
6 tablespoons water	3/4 cup cake meal, unsifted
2 1/2 teaspoons grated lemon rind	3/4 cup potato starch, unsifted

Beat egg yolks with water, lemon juice and sugar until light and fluffy (3 minutes at medium speed). Gradually add cake meal, potato starch and lemon rind and continue beating for an additional 2 minutes. Beat egg whites with salt until very firm peaks form. Fold egg whites into batter gently but thoroughly. Pour into an ungreased 10 inch tube pan and bake in 350 degree oven for approximately 1 hour. Check at 45 minutes. If top springs back when touched, remove and invert until cooled.

Maureen Chodosh

Passover Sponge Cake

12 eggs, separated
2³/₄ cups sugar
2 cups cake meal
2 heaping tablespoons potato
    starch

¹/₂ cup orange juice and lemon
    and orange rind, grated
1 teaspoon oil

Beat whites until firm and sticks to bowl turned upside down. Gradually add sugar and beat until not gritty. Beat yolks and add juice, rind, and oil. Beat well. Add yolk mix to whites. Beat until well blended. Fold in cake meal and potato starch. Pour into paper lined 9x13 inch pan. Bake at 325 degrees for 45 minutes. Turn oven up to 350 degrees and bake 10 minutes more.

Meryl Peters-Ehrlich

Although my husband's mother passed away several years before we met, I am fortunate to have a sister-in-law not only generous enough to share their mother's legacy with me, but willing to fly from the East Coast and bake it for us this last Passover.

She brought with her the family secret, an old Yahrzeit glass that her mother used for measuring. Of course we know that it equals one cup, but somehow it wouldn't taste the same if she didn't use it.

We used an electric hand mixer for the blending, but it took twice as long. Since then my sister-in-law sent us her mixmaster, so now we're sure she will return next Passover. My family expects this is the start of our new Passover tradition.

Our Favorite Passover Sponge Cake

10 eggs, separated
1¹/₂ cups sugar
dash of salt

5 well rounded tablespoons Passover cake meal
3 tablespoons potato starch
¹/₄ cup lemonade

Sift sugar, cake meal, potato starch and salt together. Beat egg whites until stiff but not dry. Set aside. Beat egg yolks. Add sugar and lemonade to yolks and continue beating until smooth. Add flour and liquids to egg yolks until blended. Fold egg whites into egg yolk mixture. Consistency should be like pancake batter. Pour into tube pan and bake ¹/₂ hour at 325 degrees and ¹/₂ hour at 300 degrees. Cool before serving.

Ann Packer

Breakfast on Passover was always special for my brother and me because we were allowed to have Mom's sponge cake for breakfast. Unfortunately, we only got to eat it then. The lemonade gives it a great flavor and makes it so good you'll be tempted to serve it all year long!

Ann Packer

Passover Spice Sponge Cake

12 eggs, separated
2 cups sugar
1½ teaspoons cinnamon
⅓ cup kosher grape wine

¼ teaspoon cloves
1½ cups matzo cake flour
1 cup blanched almonds, chopped

Beat egg yolks and sugar until very light. Add spices, wine, nuts and cake meal. Fold in stiffly beaten egg whites. Bake in moderate oven at 325 degrees for about an hour.

Mrs. Paul Dublin

Passover Apple Torte

6 large eggs, separated, at room temperature
2 cups plus 1 tablespoon sugar
¾ cups matzo cake meal
¾ cup potato starch
1 cup apple juice

1 tablespoon grated lemon rind
½ teaspoon vanilla
3 large Granny Smith green apples
1 teaspoon cinnamon

In a large bowl beat the yolks until they are thick and pale; add 1¾ cups of the sugar gradually, and beat the mixture until it is very thick.

Into a small bowl sift together the matzo cake meal and the potato starch and add the mixture to the yolk mixture alternately with the apple juice, beginning and ending with the matzo mixture and blending the mixture after each addition. Add the rind and the vanilla and beat the mixture until it is combined well.

Beat the whites until they hold soft peaks, add ¼ cup of the remaining sugar, a little at a time, beating until they just hold stiff peaks. Stir in ½ cup of the whites into the apple juice mixture and fold in the remaining whites gently but thoroughly.

Pour the batter into a greased 9x13 inch baking pan, spreading it evenly, and arrange apple slices over it, overlapping slightly. In a small bowl stir together the remaining 1 tablespoon of sugar and the cinnamon and sprinkle the mixture over the apples. Bake in the middle of a preheated 325 degree oven for 50 to 55 minutes.

Joyce Kurtz

Passover Apple Cake

³/₄ cup sugar
¹/₃ cup oil
3 eggs
³/₄ cup cake matzo meal
5 apples, peeled and sliced

Topping:
¹/₃ cup chopped walnuts
¹/₂ cup sugar
2 teaspoons cinnamon

Beat sugar and oil. Add eggs, one at a time, beating after each one. Stir in cake matzo meal.

In a small bowl, mix topping ingredients. Use an 8 or 9 inch square pan. Grease. Put in the pan a layer of batter, layer of apples, layer of batter, layer of apples and finally topping mix. Bake at 350 degrees for 45 minutes. The batter will be thinly spread.

Gail Bates

Passover Rhubarb Cobbler

1³/₄ cups sugar
¹/₄ cup quick cooking tapioca
4 cups rhubarb, ¹/₂ inch pieces
1 cup fresh or frozen
    unsweetened raspberries

2 tablespoons lemon juice
1 cup matzo meal
¹/₂ cup margarine
¹/₈ teaspoon nutmeg

In a shallow 1¹/₂ to 2 quart glass bowl mix 1¹/₄ cups sugar, tapioca and add rhubarb, raspberries and lemon juice. Mix gently but thoroughly. Let stand 15 minutes to 1 hour to soften tapioca. Mix several times.

In a food processor or bowl, whirl or rub together with your fingers the matzo meal, the remaining ¹/₂ cup sugar, margarine and nutmeg until fine crumbs form. Squeeze to compact into lumps then crumble over the rhubarb mixture. Bake in a 375 degree oven until bubbling in center, about 1 hour.

Serves 6 to 8.

Passover Chocolate Nut Torte

6 eggs, separated
1½ cups sugar
1 cup chopped walnuts
4 ounces semi-sweet
   chocolate, grated fine

2 red Delicious apples, cored
   and grated
½ cup cake matzo meal

Preheat oven to 350 degrees. Beat egg yolks with sugar until thick (2 minutes on high speed). Gently stir in walnuts, chocolate, apples and matzo meal. Beat egg whites until stiff. Fold into mixture. Bake in greased 9 inch springform pan for 1 hour. Cool in pan. Remove and dust top with powdered sugar before serving.

Diana Rosenthal

Passover Nut Cake

8 eggs, separated
1½ cups sugar
⅓ cup Passover wine
⅓ cup orange juice

1¼ cups cake matzo meal
½ teaspoon cinnamon
⅓ cup finely ground almonds

Beat egg yolks until thick and lemon colored. Add sugar gradually, beating until mixture is light colored but very thick. Add wine and orange juice. Beat for 3 minutes. Sift the cake matzo meal, salt and cinnamon three times. Add finely ground almonds. Fold the dry ingredients lightly into the egg yolks. Beat the egg whites until stiff but not dry. Fold into cake batter, blending well. Pour into a 10 inch springform pan. Bake in a slow oven at 300 to 325 degrees for about 1 hour, or until done.

Siglinde Applebaum

Passover Farfel Cookies

2 cups sifted cake meal
2 cups farfel
1 cup chopped walnuts
1¹/₂ cups sugar

1 teaspoon cinnamon
1 cup oil
4 beaten eggs

Mix all ingredients together. Roll into balls. Flatten with fork and bake on a lightly greased cookie sheet 25 to 30 minutes in a 350 degree oven.

Makes about 4 dozen.

Lynne Sneiderman

Passover Brownies

3³/₄ ounces bittersweet
    chocolate
¹/₄ cup butter
2 eggs

¹/₈ teaspoon salt
²/₃ cup sugar
¹/₂ cup cake meal
¹/₂ cup nuts, chopped

Melt chocolate and butter in the top of a double boiler. Beat the eggs with salt until thick. Add sugar, cake meal, and nuts. Fold in chocolate mixture. Pour into a greased 8 inch square pan. Bake at 325 degrees for 20 minutes. Cut while hot into squares. Guaranteed to be a hit!! May not even reach the table.

Maureen Chodosh

How to Cook a Husband

Husbands will be very tender and delicious when served as follows. Get a large jar, called the Jar of Faithfulness (which all good wives keep on hand). Place your husband in it and set him near the fire of conjugal love. Let the fire be pretty warm and above all let the heat be constant. Cover him with affection, kindness and garnish with modesty becoming familiarity and spiced with pleasantness. And if you add kisses and other confectioneries, let them be accompanied with sufficient portions of secrecy mixed with prudence and moderation. I would like all good wives to try this recipe and realize what an admirable dish a husband makes when properly cooked.

Anna Shelkowsky

Baked Goods

Lag B'Omer

The ancient grain harvest was celebrated by bringing a measure, or omer, of grain to the Temple. Various reasons are given for the seven week period between Passover and Shavuot being a period of semi-mourning. Some say a plague occurred during this period resulting in the sorrowful time. For whatever reason, Lag B'Omer in the midst breaks the atmosphere. Festivities are encouraged and picnics, barbecues, dancing and the lighting of bonfires accompany the celebration. Traditionally, a boy's first hair cut, at the age of three, will occur on Lag B'Omer.

No special foods are associated with the holiday other than picnic foods, cakes, bagels, sandwiches and cookies. In Israel chick peas, falafel, fruits and nuts are popular fare.

Shavuot

Ushering in summer, Shavuot is a spring harvest festival and one of the three great pilgrimage festivals when one was required to attend worship at the Temple in Jerusalem. It is traditionally the birthday of the Torah and celebrates the giving of the Law at Mount Sinai. It concludes the spring cycle of holidays that began with the counting of the Omer, a new sheaf of barley offered at the Temple, on the second day of Passover. Traditionally the Book of Ruth is read on Shavuot. Set against the background of a harvest festival it tells of a non-Jewish woman who became not only one of the Jewish people, but the one from whose family King David came. It symbolizes both the ingathering of the harvest and the gathering in of the people to the Law. First fruits and cheese blintzes and other dairy foods are eaten in honor of the Law which is compared to "milk and honey".

What is...

CHALLAH *is an Eastern Yiddish name for a special loaf of bread baked fresh for the Sabbath. This tradition is so widespread among world Jewish communities that it may have had its roots in the Talmudic era. Over the centuries, the bread has assumed a variety of sizes, shapes and ingredients, depending on the customs of each region. Today we are accustomed to a braided loaf that was adopted by the German Jews in the 16th and 17th centuries.*

Diana's Challah

2 packages dried yeast
2 tablespoons sugar
1½ cups warm water
1½ teaspoons salt

2 tablespoons shortening
2 eggs and 1 egg yolk, beaten
1 egg white, for wash
6 cups all-purpose flour

Dissolve yeast in a large bowl with warm water and sugar. Add 2 cups of flour, salt, shortening, eggs and yolk. Beat until smooth. Stir in 2 more cups of flour until all flour is incorporated. Repeat with 1 more cup of flour. Dough should be holding into a ball. If not, add ½ cup more flour. When dough is a ball, turn out on a floured board or cloth and knead until smooth and the ball will hold its shape. Return to a clean, greased bowl, cover and let rise in a warm place (you may prewarm an oven to 150 degrees, turn it off and let the dough rise there).

When dough has doubled in size (about 1 to 2 hours) turn out on floured surface. Cut into 4 pieces. Roll 3 of the pieces into sausage shapes about 14 inches long and braid. Cut remaining piece into 3 small pieces and make a small braid to place on the big braid. Place loaf on a greased baking sheet, cover and rest for ½ hour.

Preheat oven to 350 degrees. Before baking brush loaf with egg white (beaten with 1 teaspoon of water). You can also sprinkle with poppy or sesame seeds. Bake 45 minutes or until brown and hollow sounding when thumped on bottom.

Diana Rosenthal

Deborah's Challah

2 packages active dry yeast
3/4 cup water, very warm
1 tablespoon sugar
1 teaspoon salt
2 eggs, lightly beaten
2 tablespoons vegetable oil
3 cups white unbleached flour

1/2 to 3/4 cup stone ground
  whole wheat flour
poppy seeds
Egg Glaze:
1 egg yolk, beaten
1/4 teaspoon water

Dissolve the yeast in the water in a large bowl. When dissolved, add sugar, salt, eggs and oil. Stir in as much flour as you can, then turn out onto a floured surface; knead in the rest of the flour. Knead until the dough is smooth and elastic (about 10 minutes). Place the dough in a lightly oiled bowl, cover and leave in a warm place until it has doubled in size.

Take dough out of bowl and knead about 1 minute to smooth it into a ball. Divide the dough in 3 equal portions. Roll each of the 3 portions into a rope about 10 inches long. Pinch the 3 ropes together at one end and braid together. Place the braided load on a non-stick cookie sheet and let it rest, covered, until it doubles in size.

Brush with egg glaze and sprinkle with poppy seeds. Bake 10 minutes in a preheated 400 degree oven, then reduce oven to 375 degrees and bake 35 to 40 minutes longer. This makes a very large loaf or two smaller loaves (to do so reduce baking time by 5 to 7 minutes). The extra loaf can go into the freezer for that busy day when you don't have time to bake.

Deborah Smolen

Kids' Challah

If you don't have time to make or get fresh challah on Friday night, use refrigerated breadstick dough. Have the children twist three breadsticks together, bake and presto, the children have made challah.

Challahs come in many shapes and sizes. For the average family a one pound braided challah might be just enough. But what could be more beautiful than a ten pound braided challah made for special celebrations. Challahs braided with three or five braids are those seen most often. For Rosh Hashanah spiral challahs are made to symbolize the desire for a long life. In eastern Europe these round Rosh Hashanah challahs had a dough ring formed on the top to symbolize the hope for a complete and harmonious year. For Shavuot, which commemorates the giving of the Torah, a challah might have a ladder on top to symbolize the ascent to heaven. In the Ukraine a bird's head would be shaped from dough and placed on top of the round challah, symbolizing the phrase in Isaiah, "as birds hovering, so will the Lord of Hosts protect Jerusalem." A round challah with a hand was created in Volhynia on Hoshana Rabba symbolizing that, on this the seventh day of Sukkot, the judgement passed by God on Yom Kippur is confirmed by a written verdict and the hand of man is extended to receive it. A dough key was placed on an oval challah in Volhynia for the first Sabbath after Passover. The key symbolized the gate of release which traditionally remains open for a month after the festival. Jews from Lithuania baked challahs topped with a crown in accordance with the words "Let all crown God." In Rhodes, challahs, called coulouri, are shaped in a ring.

My mother always remembered her Grandmother holding a loaf of bread up to her chest to cut a slice and cutting towards her body. Though her Grandmother was a wonderful baker, it made getting a slice of bread a little harrowing.

Joyce Kurtz

Dilly Bread

¹/₄ cup melted butter or
  margarine
3 tablespoons chopped
  parsley
2 tablespoons lemon juice

1 egg, beaten
1 teaspoon dillweed
2 packages refrigerated
  buttermilk biscuits

Combine butter, parsley, lemon juice and dillweed. Dip biscuits in mixture. Stand on end in a greased 5¹/₂ cup ring mold. Brush the tops with beaten eggs and bake at 375 degrees for 12 to 15 minutes.

Judy Reibel

Mandel Bread

3 cups sifted flour
1 cup sugar
1 tablespoon almond extract
3 eggs, lightly beaten

1 stick plus 1 tablespoon
  melted butter, cooled
2 teaspoons baking powder
1 teaspoon vanilla
2 cups chopped walnuts

Mix butter and sugar well. Add eggs. Add vanilla and almond extract. Slowly add sifted flour and baking powder. Mix in nuts. Butter 3 small loaf pans (or ice cube trays) and divide mixtures. Bake at 350 degrees for 30 minutes or until done. Cool, loosen, slice and put back in oven on cookie sheets to brown.

Judy Reibel

What is...

BAGELS were first mentioned in 1610 in the ordinances of Cracow, Poland, which stated that they should be sent as gifts to women about to give birth and to midwives. It is believed they originated in southern Germany or Austria and possibly were related to the medieval pretzel. Nowadays few take the time to make their own bagels since there are good bagel bakeries in most communities.

Mom's Favorite Mandel Bread

walnuts, as many as you like
3 eggs
1 teaspoon orange extract
1/2 cup oil

1 cup sugar
3 cups flour
1/2 teaspoon baking soda
sugar and cinnamon mixture

Mix sugar and eggs until light. Add oil and orange extract. Combine flour and baking soda and add gradually, followed by the walnuts. Divide in 4 pieces and form into long rolls. Twist and flatten. Place rolls on an oiled baking sheet. Bake for 15 to 20 minutes in a 350 degree oven. Remove from the oven and while still warm slice on the diagonal and sprinkle with the sugar and cinnamon mixture. Place back in the oven for an additional 15 minutes or until nicely browned.

Shaaron Delsohn

The Greatest Blueberry Muffins

1 egg
1/2 cup milk
1/4 cup salad oil
1 1/2 cups flour

1/2 cup sugar
2 teaspoons baking powder
1/2 teaspoon salt
1 cup blueberries

Beat egg slightly with a fork. Stir in milk and salad oil. Sift together and then add flour, sugar, baking powder and salt. Stir in blueberries. Bake 20 to 25 minutes in a 400 degree oven.

Makes 1 dozen muffins.

Joyce Kurtz

Mandel Bread with a Kick

2 cups flour
1 teaspoon baking soda
1 cup sugar
dash of salt
3 eggs, beaten very well

1/2 teaspoon vanilla
1/4 cup brandy or rum
6 ounces almonds, chopped
  coarsely

Mix the dry ingredients, add liquids. Separate into 2 sections and with hands, form two long rolls about 2 inches wide, on a cookie sheet. Bake in a preheated 300 degree oven for about 35 to 50 minutes, until lightly browned. While hot, slice rolls into diagonal slices about 1/2 inch thick. Brown on both sides in the oven, for a few minutes, until as brown as desired. The longer the time spent in the oven, the drier the Mandel Bread becomes.

Sonja Ehrlich

Oatmeal Bread

1 1/2 cups warm water
1 package dried yeast
2 tablespoons brown sugar or
  molasses
1/2 cup powdered milk

1 1/2 cups rolled oats
2 teaspoons salt
1/3 cup oil
3 to 4 cups flour (white, whole
  wheat, or a combination)

Dissolve yeast in large bowl with warm water and sugar. Add two cups of flour and powdered milk. Stir well and let sit 10 to 15 minutes until yeast starts to bubble. Add oats, salt, and oil and mix well. Stir in flour 1 cup at a time until dough forms a stiff ball. Knead on a floured surface until smooth. Cover and rest for 1 hour. Punch down and briefly knead dough before placing in a greased loaf pan. Allow to rise again. Bake in 350 degree oven for 35 to 40 minutes. Top should be brown. Serve with honey and butter.

Diana Rosenthal

Rugelach

½ pound margarine
½ pound cream cheese
2 cups flour

brown sugar, nuts and
cinnamon

Cream margarine and cream cheese and gradually add flour. Roll into a ball and chill overnight. Divide ball into 2 pieces and roll each into an ⅛ inch thick oblong. Mix brown sugar, ½ as much nuts and cinnamon until a rich brown color. Liberally spread brown sugar mix on dough and roll jelly roll fashion. Cut ¾ inch slices and bake on a greased baking sheet in a 350 degree oven for 20 minutes or until brown and bubbling. This is the famous Jewish Food Festival recipe enjoyed by all!

Joyce Kurtz

Chocolate Zucchini Bread

2½ cups flour
½ cup cocoa
2½ teaspoons baking powder
1½ teaspoons baking soda
1 teaspoon salt
1 teaspoon cinnamon
¾ cup butter or margarine
2 cups sugar

3 eggs
2 teaspoons vanilla
2 teaspoons grated orange
   peel
2 cups shredded zucchini
½ cup milk
1 cup chopped walnuts

Combine flour, cocoa, baking powder, baking soda, salt, cinnamon and set aside. Mix butter and sugar. Add eggs, milk and dry ingredients. Mix. With spoon, stir in vanilla, orange peel and zucchini. Add nuts and milk. Pour into 10 inch tube pan or 2 loaf pans. Bake at 350 degrees for 40 to 60 minutes or until toothpick comes out clean.

Maxine Suval

No Beat Popovers

2 eggs	1 cup sifted flour
1 cup milk	½ teaspoon salt

Grease 1 muffin pan (6 large or 12 small cups in a pan). Break eggs into a mixing bowl and add the remaining ingredients. Mix well with a spoon, disregarding lumps. Fill cups ¾ full. Set oven at 450 degrees and immediately put in the muffin pan. Bake 30 minutes and serve at once. **Do not preheat oven and do not open oven during baking.**

JoAnne Rockower

Ruth's Mandel Brot

¾ cup oil	3 eggs
1 cup sugar	¾ cup jam
3 cups flour	¾ cup raisins
2 teaspoons baking powder	½ cup chopped nuts
1 teaspoon vanilla	cinnamon and sugar mix

Mix together the oil, sugar, flour, baking powder, vanilla and eggs to form a fairly stiff dough. Divide the dough into 3 equal balls. Flatten out each ball in turn on floured wax paper. Roll into a rectangle, ½ inch thick.

Spread each rectangle with ⅓ of the jam, raisins and nuts. Roll like a jelly roll, using the wax paper to roll with. Sprinkle the top with cinnamon and sugar. Bake at 350 degrees for 50 to 60 minutes or until lightly brown.

Important: Slice hot.

Elaine Halprin

Annie's Strudel

1 pound chopped walnuts,
  powdered
1 can whole cranberries
3 eggs, separated
1 pound pitted prunes,
  ground
3 cups or more flour
1 tablespoon vinegar
1 lemon, juice and rind

bread, cake or cookie crumbs
  (a few handfuls)
2 tablespoons baking powder
1/4 cup warm water
3 tablespoons oil
1 1/2 cups sugar
8 apples, thinly sliced
1 cup or more raisins
cinnamon and sugar mixture

Sift together dry ingredients. Add 3 egg whites. Add water, oil, vinegar and sugar. Knead until elastic in bowl. Then knead on board generously floured until dough is easy to handle and stretches. Cut in 4 pieces, knead in more flour if necessary. Roll out each piece until it is thin.

Peel and slice apples. Put lots of oil in long pans. Stretch dough out on a table cloth or waxed paper. Cut away rough edges. Wipe on lemon and add oil to cover all dough.

Generously sprinkle cinnamon and sugar. Sprinkle on crumbs and nuts. Spread out raisins, prunes on 1 side of dough. Put cranberries on top of the prunes. Add apples on top of this. Roll up tightly. Put in pan and stroke with egg yolks mixed with water. Slit the dough and bake 350 degrees for 50 to 60 minutes.

Elaine Halprin

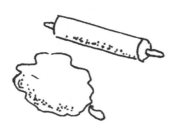

> ### What is...
>
> HAMANTASCHEN, three cornered cakes filled with poppy seeds and of German origin, were prepared in Eastern Europe on Purim. The name was derived from mohn (poppy seed) and taschen (pockets).

Hamantaschen

1 cup butter, room
   temperature
2 cups sugar
2 eggs
4 teaspoons baking powder
4 cups flour
4 teaspoons orange juice
2 teaspoons vanilla
1 egg for egg wash
Prune Filling:
1 cup pitted prunes
$2/3$ cup raisins

$1^{1}/_{3}$ cups prune butter or a
   good plum jam
$1/2$ cup grated coconut
$2/3$ cup chopped walnuts
Poppy Seed Filling:
2 cups poppy seeds
2 cups milk
$1/2$ cup raisins or currants
$1/4$ cup chopped almonds
4 tablespoons butter
$1/4$ cup light corn syrup
1 teaspoon vanilla

Cream butter and sugar until smooth. Add eggs and mix well. Sift together flour and baking powder. Combine juice and vanilla. Add flour and liquids alternately to butter mixture. Refrigerate at least $1/2$ hour. Divide dough in 2 pieces. Roll each piece on a floured board or cloth to a thickness of $1/4$ inch. Cut into 3 inch circles, placing a teaspoon of the filling of your choice in the center. Pinch closed in triangle shape leaving a small opening in the center. Beat egg with a little water and brush on hamantaschen. Bake on a greased sheet at 350 degrees for 20 to 25 minutes or until lightly brown. This recipe can be easily frozen and reheated. For quick fillings use fruit jams combined with chopped nuts for more body.

Prune Filling: Plump prunes and raisins in hot water. Drain and puree with prune butter. Add remaining ingredients being careful not to over process.

Poppy Seed Filling: Place all ingredients in a saucepan. Bring to a boil and simmer over medium heat until thick and milk is absorbed.

Diana Rosenthal

Edna's Cookies

3 cups flour
1 cup sugar
2 teaspoons baking powder
1 cup shortening
2 eggs
1½ teaspoons vanilla

4 ounces pineapple tidbits
and juice
1 cup or more raisins
½ cup coconut, optional
cinnamon and sugar mix

Mix flour, sugar and baking powder. Cut in shortening, eggs and vanilla. Add pineapple and juice and mix. Add more juice to mixture until the batter won't stick to your fingers. Add raisins and coconut and mix. Form small balls (about 1 inch) and roll in cinnamon and sugar mix. Bake at 350 degrees about 20 minutes. Cookies will be a light brown on top. Danger: These are habit forming!

Elaine Halprin

Peanut Cookies

1 cup margarine
1 cup sugar
1 cup brown sugar
2 eggs
2 teaspoons vanilla
2 cups flour

1 teaspoon baking soda
1 teaspoon baking powder
1 cup roasted, salted Spanish
peanuts
1 cup oatmeal
1 cup corn flakes

Mix ingredients. Drop by teaspoonfuls onto greased baking pan. Bake at 350 degrees for 10 to 12 minutes.

Gail and Dennis Bates

Marta's Cookies
(Blaetter Teig)

2 cups flour   **8 ounces cream cheese**
3 egg yolks   **2 cubes sweet margarine**

Cream cream cheese and margarine, add egg yolks and gradually add flour. Refrigerate dough overnight. Cut dough in half and return unused half to refrigerator. Roll dough 1/4 inch thick and cut into rounds approximately 2½ inches in diameter. Make cookie sandwiches by using 2 rounds of dough and filling them with either raspberry jam or marmalade. Sprinkle cookie sheet with flour. Brush cookies with egg yolk and sprinkle with sugar. Bake until light brown, about 20 to 25 minutes at 350 degrees.

Marta Weltsch

These cookies were a special treat for our whole congregation while Sam and Marta Weltsch were alive. We all were delighted when Sam and Marta attended an event, and they attended everything. They were the grandparents of us all, warm and always interested in everything and everyone. Marta never went anywhere without bringing either her cheesecake or these wonderful cookies. Sam gave us this recipe for Come to the Table *but said no one would be able to make them like Marta. Please try this recipe and prove Sam wrong.*

Strudel

¼ pound butter	bread crumbs
¼ pound margarine	nuts
1 egg yolk	raisins
1 cup sour cream	cinnamon
2 cups flour	1 egg white
apricot preserves or cherry pineapple preserves	powdered sugar

Cream butter and margarine with egg yolk. Mix in sour cream and flour. Make a ball; wrap in waxed paper and put in coldest part of refrigerator overnight. Roll out on floured board very thin. Sprinkle with nuts, raisins and cinnamon. Make a thin layer of preserves over the nuts, raisins and cinnamon. Sprinkle lightly with bread crumbs. Roll up in a long strip. Spread top with egg white. Bake on ungreased cookie sheet at 350 degrees until light brown.

Same dough may be used to make Rugelach. Cut into squares and sprinkle with sugar, cinnamon, nuts and raisins. Roll up from a corner and form into crescent shape. Dip into egg white and then into sugar and cinnamon. Bake at 350 degrees until light brown.

Joyce Fischbein

Strudel

2 cups flour	raisins
1 small carton cottage cheese	shredded coconut
¾ cup shortening	chopped nuts
Filling:	Topping:
jam	cinnamon
sugar	sugar
cinnamon	milk

Blend first three ingredients with hands and shape into 4 balls. Roll in waxed paper and refrigerate overnight. Roll balls separately as thin as possible. Fill each section, roll, flour and pinch ends. Brush tops with cinnamon, sugar and milk. Make slits for later cutting (do not cut through). Bake at 350 degrees for 20 to 30 minutes. Cool and cut into pieces.

Norma Robinson

Mom's Plum Kuchen

4 tablespoons butter
1 cup flour
1 egg
prune plums

½ teaspoon baking powder
¼ cup sugar
2 tablespoons milk

Cut butter into dry ingredients. Add egg and then milk. Butter and flour a springform pan. You also may use a 9 inch square pan. Pat dough to line bottom of pan. Keep flouring fingers.

Quarter plums. You also may use apples, nectarines or apricots. Sprinkle sugar, cinnamon and nutmeg on them. Line the dough with the fruit, setting it in neat rows or in circular patterns. Mix 1 egg yolk and 3 tablespoons milk, beating lightly. Pour over the fruit. Bake for 20 to 30 minutes in a 400 degree oven.

Joyce Kurtz

My Mother's Jewish Apple Cake

5 to 6 apples, peeled and
    sliced
5 tablespoons sugar
2 teaspoons cinnamon
3 cups flour
3 teaspoons baking powder

1 teaspoon salt (optional)
1 cup oil
2 cups sugar
¼ cup orange juice
1 tablespoon vanilla
4 eggs

Sprinkle 5 tablespoons sugar and 2 teaspoons cinnamon on apples and set aside. Sift together 3 cups flour, 3 teaspoons baking powder, and salt. Cream oil and 2 cups sugar. Add orange juice, vanilla, eggs and flour mixture to sugar mixture. Grease tube pan. Pour ½ batter in pan, top with ½ apples. Add rest of batter, then rest of apples. Bake at 325 degrees for 2 hours until brown. Cover lightly with foil after 1 hour to prevent over-browning. Cool overnight in upright position. Freezes well.

Ellen Krause

Linzer Torte

1½ cups almonds, unblanched
½ cup butter or margarine,
   plus 2 teaspoons
⅔ cup sugar
2 cups flour, unsifted
1 egg
½ teaspoon vanilla
½ teaspoon lemon peel,
   grated
½ teaspoon baking powder

Fruit Filling:
6 cups fruit (any fresh berries
   such as strawberries,
   ollalieberries, blueberries,
   etc.) or peaches, plums,
   apricots or nectarines
¾ to 1¼ cups sugar,
   depending on sweetness
   of fruit
1 tablespoon lemon juice
1 stick cinnamon (optional)

In a blender or food processor, whirl nuts until finely ground. Put aside. Beat butter and sugar until light and fluffy. Add egg, vanilla and lemon peel. Beat to blend. Stir together flour, baking powder and ground nuts. Gradually add to creamed mixture, beating well. (If you have a heavy duty mixer, beat in all flour-nut mixture; otherwise stir in mixture with spoon.) Cover and chill at least 30 minutes, but it will wait overnight.

To form crust, divide dough into thirds. Return ⅓ to refrigerator and press remaining dough evenly over bottom and sides of a 12 inch tort pan with removable bottom, or a 12 inch pizza pan.

Fruit Filling: Place 6 cups of fruit in saucepan. Depending on sweetness of fruit, add ¾ to 1¼ cups of sugar, 1 tablespoon of lemon juice and 1 stick of cinnamon (optional). Boil quickly, stirring frequently to prevent sticking, over low to medium-low heat until jam is thick and reduced to about 2 cups. This takes 45 minutes to 1 hour. Discard cinnamon stick. (As a short cut, begin with jam; heat, add 1 tablespoon lemon juice and cinnamon stick.)

Spread filling over dough. With reserved third of dough, gently roll strips about ¼ inch thick on lightly floured board. Form lattice over top. If strip breaks, just pinch back together. Bake at 350 degrees for 30 minutes or until crust is lightly browned.

Joyce Kurtz

My most prized possession is my grandmother's old cookbook, dated 1936, complete with torn binding and food-stained pages. There are handwritten recipes in the front and the back, including "Clarice's divinity" from my mother's older sister and "Butter's carrot pudding."

Affectionately called "Butter," Mrs. Butterbaugh was my grandmother's best friend. She was a wonderfully round and joyful woman and it was years before I ever learned that her real name wasn't Mrs. Butterball.

I inherited several traits from my mother's mother, including my sturdy body build and certain "endowments." (Granny always had the softest chest to rest my head on.)

From looking at her cookbook, I must have also inherited her love of sweets. Most of her handwritten recipes were for desserts. Maybe that's why I remember her apple pie and the cookie jar on her kitchen table the most.

Barbara Quinn

Very Quick Apple Cake

2 cups green apples, cubed
1 egg
1 cup sugar
1/4 cup oil
1 teaspoon vanilla
1 cup flour
1 teaspoon baking soda
1/2 teaspoon cinnamon
1 cup chopped nuts

Break egg over the apples and stir. Blend in the sugar, oil, and vanilla. Mix flour, baking soda and cinnamon and add to the apple mixture. Add nuts. Pour into greased 8x8 inch baking dish and bake for 25 minutes in a 325 degree oven. This is best served within a few hours of baking.

Joyce Kurtz

Easy as Pie
Apple Cake

5 cups peeled sliced green apples
1⅓ cups sugar
2 teaspoons ground cinnamon

½ cup butter or margarine
1 cup flour
2 eggs

Place apples in 9 inch pie plate. Combine ⅓ cup sugar and 2 teaspoons cinnamon. Sprinkle all but 2 teaspoons cinnamon sugar mixture on top of apples. In bowl cream butter and remaining 1 cup sugar. Add flour and eggs. Spread mixture over apples. Top with reserved 2 teaspoons cinnamon sugar. Bake at 325 degrees 1 hour and 10 minutes. When done cake will not be firm.

Makes 1 (9 inch) pie.

Kerry Beren

Applesauce Loaf Cake

½ cup margarine
1 cup sugar
1 egg
1 cup unsweetened applesauce
1¾ cups flour, sifted

1½ teaspoons cinnamon
1 teaspoon nutmeg
¼ teaspoon cloves
½ teaspoon salt
1 teaspoon baking soda

Cream margarine and sugar. Add egg. Beat and then add applesauce. Mix and sift in remaining ingredients. Bake in pan for 35 minutes at 350 degrees.

Gail Bates

Pineapple Surprise Cake

1 (20 ounce) can crushed
  pineapple, drain, but save
  liquid
3/4 cup chopped walnuts
1/4 cup sugar
1 1/2 teaspoons cinnamon
2 3/4 cups cake flour

2 1/4 teaspoons baking powder
1/4 teaspoon salt
1 1/2 cups sugar
1/2 pound butter or margarine
3/4 cup pineapple juice
2 teaspoons vanilla
4 eggs, at room temperature

Combine walnuts, cinnamon and 1/4 cup sugar together and set aside. Sift together (twice) flour, baking powder and salt. Cream butter and 1 1/2 cups sugar together. Add dry sifted ingredients alternating with pineapple juice to butter mixture. Beat together for 2 minutes. Add eggs and vanilla and beat an additional 2 minutes. Pour mixture into lightly greased cake pan. Add spoonfuls of pineapple, nut and cinnamon mixture around top of batter. Bake in 375 degree oven for 45 to 50 minutes. Cool before serving.

Ann Packer

Boston Bathtub Fudge Cake

1/4 pound margarine
1 cup sugar
4 eggs
1 large can dark chocolate
  syrup
1 cup flour
1 teaspoon baking powder

1 teaspoon vanilla
Icing:
1/2 box powdered sugar
2 squares bitter chocolate,
  melted
1 teaspoon vanilla
sour cream or other liquid

Cream margarine and sugar. Add eggs one at a time. Add chocolate syrup and vanilla. Mix dry ingredients together and gradually add to chocolate mixture. Place in oiled and floured 9x13 inch glass dish. Bake 25 to 30 minutes at 350 degrees.

Icing: Blend ingredients in sour cream or other liquid to make creamy and thick. Pour over cooled cake.

Terry Chaplan

Esther's Coffee Cake

1/4 pound butter or margarine	1 cup sour cream
1 cup sugar	1 teaspoon vanilla
2 eggs, beaten	apple slices (optional)
2 cups flour	Crunch:
1 teaspoon baking powder	1/2 cup nuts, chopped
1 teaspoon baking soda	1/2 cup sugar
1/4 teaspoon salt	1 teaspoon cinnamon

Cream butter with sugar. Add beaten eggs and blend. Sift together flour, baking powder, baking soda and salt. Add dry ingredients to creamed mixture alternately with sour cream which has been blended with vanilla. Turn half of the batter into a greased tube pan, sprinkle half of the crunch over it, add the rest of batter and top with remaining crunch. (Optional: press apple slices around top then sprinkle crunch). Bake at 350 degrees for 45 minutes.

Beverly G. Bean

My Italian Grandmother's Jewish Coffee Cake

8 ounces sour cream	Topping:
1 teaspoon baking soda	1/2 stick butter
1 stick butter	1/2 cup flour
1 cup sugar	4 tablespoons brown sugar
2 eggs	4 tablespoons sugar
1/4 teaspoon salt	1/2 teaspoon cinnamon
1 teaspoon vanilla	1/4 teaspoon salt
1 1/2 cups flour, sifted	1/2 teaspoon baking powder
1 teaspoon baking powder	1/2 cup walnuts, chopped

Mix sour cream and baking soda and let stand. Cream butter and sugar. Add eggs, one at a time, beating well after each one. Add salt, vanilla, and sour cream mixture. Mix well. Add flour and baking powder. Beat well. Mix all topping ingredients with pastry blender until butter is crumbly. Pour 1/2 cake mix into 9x13 inch pan and cover with 1/2 topping. Add rest of cake mix and finish with rest of topping. Bake at 350 degrees for 40 to 45 minutes.

Katherine Penebre

Judy's Coffee Cake

1 cup sugar
1/4 pound butter
2 eggs
8 ounces sour cream
2 cups flour
1 teaspoon soda

1 teaspoon baking powder
1 teaspoon vanilla
1/2 cup brown sugar
1 small package chocolate
   chips
1/2 cup nuts

Cream together butter, sugar, eggs and sour cream. Sift dry ingredients together and add to the first mixture along with the vanilla.

Combine brown sugar, chocolate chips and nuts together to make the filling. Grease and flour an angel food cake pan. Pour in a little less than half of the batter. Sprinkle with a little less than half the filling. Add the remaining batter and top with the remaining filling. Bake at 350 degrees for 45 to 50 minutes.

Judy Reibel

Bea's Sour Cream Cake

3 eggs
1 cup shortening or 1/2 pound
   butter
1 cup sugar
1/2 pint sour cream
3 teaspoons baking powder

1 teaspoon baking soda
2 3/4 cups sifted flour
Topping:
1/4 cup brown sugar
2 teaspoons cinnamon
1/4 cup chopped walnuts

Sift together the baking powder, baking soda and sifted flour. Set aside. Cream the butter. Add sugar, eggs (1 at a time). When mixed, add alternating parts of flour mixture and sour cream, starting and ending with the flour mixture. Pour half of the batter in a greased springform pan. Add 2/3 of the topping mixture. Cover with remaining batter. Drag a knife through the batter making an "S" design to create a marble effect. Sprinkle remaining topping over batter. Bake at 325 degrees for 55 minutes.

Andrea Carter

Spicy Marble Coffee Cake

½ cup margarine
¾ cup sugar
1 egg
2 cups flour
2 teaspoons baking powder
½ teaspoon salt
¾ cup milk
2 tablespoons molasses
1 teaspoon cinnamon

¼ teaspoon nutmeg
½ teaspoon ground cloves
Nut Topping Mix:
½ cup brown sugar
½ cup walnuts
2 tablespoons flour
1 teaspoon cinnamon
2 tablespoons butter, melted

Cream shortening and sugar. Add egg and beat well. Sift flour, baking powder and salt. Add to creamed mixture, alternating with milk. Divide into 2 parts. To 1 part, add molasses and spices. Spoon batter alternately into greased 8 inch pan. Zigzag spatula through. Sprinkle with nut topping mix. Bake in moderate oven at 350 degrees for 40 to 45 minutes, until done.

Serves 8.

Gail Bates

Banana Cake

1 cup bananas
¼ cup sour milk
1 teaspoon vanilla
½ cup butter or margarine
1½ cups sugar

2 eggs
2¼ cups flour
½ teaspoon baking powder
¾ teaspoon baking soda
½ teaspoon salt

Mash bananas, vanilla and sour milk. In a separate bowl beat margarine or butter, add sugar and eggs one at a time. Add banana mixture. Sift dry ingredients together and add gradually. Bake in loaf pan for 30 minutes for 350 degrees.

Trudy Licht

Pflaumenkuchen

½ pound margarine
1 cup sugar
1 egg
½ teaspoon vanilla
½ teaspoon baking powder

3¼ cups flour
  (approximately)
4 pounds fresh prune plums
  (approximately)
cinnamon and sugar, to taste

Cream margarine and sugar. Add egg, vanilla and baking powder. Slowly add 2 cups flour. Add additional flour as needed until dough doesn't stick to bowl and hands. Press dough into pie plate or metal pastry pan. Add fruit, top with cinnamon and sugar. Overlap fruit if desired. (Apricots may be used instead of plums). Bake 1 hour at 350 degrees until dough is brownish. Let cool and refrigerate. Cover with foil

Dough makes 2 (8 inch) round pies.

Connie Kean

I've made this to Break the Yom Kippur fast every year for the past eighteen years. Every time I make it I recall the first time I helped a friend assemble it as we watched our infants crawl around the kitchen. It is a recipe which was made by her mother when she was alive and is so simple and delicious that I have made it ever since. The recipe is German in origin, survived the Holocaust as the family fled to America in the latter 1930's and has recently been enjoyed by many Californians.

Connie Kean

Yeast Cake

¹/₂ **pound butter**
³/₄ **teaspoon yeast**
¹/₂ **cup sour cream**
3 eggs, separated
**1 cup plus 2 tablespoons
  sugar**

2¹/₂ cups flour, unsifted
salt
¹/₂ **teaspoon vanilla**
**raisins, nuts, cinnamon and
  sugar, mixed together**

Blend together butter, yeast, sour cream, egg yolks, 2 tablespoons sugar, flour and salt and refrigerate overnight. Divide into halves or thirds and roll out the dough. Beat together 3 egg whites and gradually add 1 cup of sugar, salt and vanilla to make a meringue.

Spread the meringue mixture over the dough. Sprinkle with a mixture of sugar, cinnamon, raisins and nuts. Roll like a jelly roll. Place on a greased pan, cover and let stand 3 hours. Bake 40 minutes at 325 to 350 degrees.

Judy Reibel

Honey Cake

4 eggs
1¹/₂ cups sugar
1 cup peanut oil
1 cup honey
1 teaspoon baking soda
1 cup strong cold tea
2¹/₂ cups all-purpose flour

2 teaspoons baking powder
¹/₂ **teaspoon cinnamon**
¹/₂ **teaspoon allspice**
¹/₄ **teaspoon ground clove**
¹/₄ **teaspoon ground ginger**
juice of ¹/₂ lemon

Preheat oven to 325 degrees. Grease and line tube pan (parchment). Dissolve the baking soda in the tea. Beat eggs, sugar, oil and honey together. Add alternately the dry and wet ingredients, begin and end with dry. Pour in pan. Bake 1 hour and 15 minutes until done.

Honey Chiffon Cake

2 cups all-purpose flour,
   sifted
1 tablespoon baking powder
$^1/_4$ teaspoon baking soda
$1^1/_2$ teaspoons ground
   cinnamon
$^1/_4$ teaspoon allspice, ginger
   and nutmeg

$^1/_4$ teaspoon salt
7 large eggs, separated
$^3/_4$ cup sugar
$^2/_3$ cup honey
$^1/_2$ cup salad oil
$^2/_3$ cup strong coffee, cooled
2 tablespoons powdered
   sugar (optional)

In a small bowl, mix flour, baking powder, baking soda, cinnamon, allspice, ginger, nutmeg and salt. In a deep bowl, whip egg whites until foamy. Beating gradually add 6 tablespoons of sugar and whip until whites hold distinct peaks. Set aside.

In another bowl, whip egg yolks, honey and remaining sugar until mixture is thick and lighter in color, scraping bowl often. Beat in oil and coffee. Add flour mixture, beat to blend. Stir about $^1/_4$ of whites into batter. Gently but thoroughly fold in remaining whites.

Scrape batter into a 10 inch wide tube pan with removable rim. Smooth batter. Bake at 325 degrees until cake springs back when pressed in its center and sides begin to pull from pan, about 55 to 60 minutes. Cool cake in pan, bottom up. Support pan by setting tube over neck of a sturdy bottle. When cool, turn upright and run a thin knife between cake and pan. Lift tube and cake from pan. Slide knife between cake and pan bottom, invert cake onto a plate. Dust with powdered sugar, serve or wrap airtight and keep up to a day. Freeze to store longer.

Maxine Suval

Aunt Faye's Honey Cake

1 cup sugar	1 teaspoon baking powder
2/3 cup vegetable oil	1 teaspoon baking soda
3 eggs	1/2 teaspoon nutmeg
1 pound honey	1/2 teaspoon cinnamon
1 cup black coffee, cold	nuts and/or raisins
3 1/2 cups flour	(optional)

Combine all ingredients into one large bowl and mix well. Add nuts and raisins at end if desired. Line a 11x13 inch pan with waxed paper. Bake at 325 degrees for about 50 minutes.

Maureen Chodosh

Gingerbread

1 cup sugar	1 teaspoon salt
1 1/2 cups oil	2 teaspoons cinnamon
4 jumbo eggs	2 teaspoons ginger
1 cup molasses	1 teaspoon cloves
2 cups flour	1 teaspoon nutmeg
2 teaspoons baking soda	3 cups grated Granny Smith
2 teaspoons baking powder	or Pippin apples

Beat together sugar, oil, eggs and molasses. Mix dry ingredients and add to sugar mixture. Add apples. Bake in a large rectangular glass baking dish at 350 degrees for 30 to 45 minutes or until done.

To serve: Sauté peeled, sliced apples in butter. Add sugar, lots of cinnamon, a little water and cornstarch mixture. Slice gingerbread and top with whipped cream and sautéed apples.

Carol Gilbert

Very Berry Cake

½ cup margarine or butter
½ cup sugar
1 teaspoon vanilla
2 large eggs
1 teaspoon grated lemon peel
2 cups flour
½ cup potato starch or
　cornstarch

1 teaspoon each baking
　powder and baking soda
⅔ cup each blackberries,
　blueberries and
　raspberries
3 tablespoons sugar
1 teaspoon quick cooking
　tapioca
2 teaspoons lemon juice

In a large bowl, beat butter and sugar until smooth and fluffy. Beat in vanilla, eggs and lemon peel until well blended. In a small bowl, combine flour and potato flour, baking powder and baking soda; add to the butter mixture and stir to mix thoroughly. Press ⅔ of the dough evenly into a well buttered and floured 8 inch diameter springform pan. Mix berries, sugar, tapioca and lemon juice and fill pan. Make a decorative topping by rolling the remaining dough, a section at a time, into ½ inch diameter ropes and place on top of cake in a criss-cross pattern. Bake the cake on the bottom rack in a 350 degree oven about 40 to 45 minutes. Let cool in pan on a rack for 30 minutes, then remove sides. Sprinkle with powdered sugar.

Makes 8 to 9 servings.

Graham Cracker Brownies

2 cups graham cracker
　crumbs
1 can sweetened condensed
　milk

1 large package semi-sweet
　chocolate chips
½ cup walnuts

Mix all ingredients together and put in a greased 8x8 inch pan. Bake at 350 degrees for 22 to 25 minutes. Cut into squares as soon as removed from oven. Remove from pan when cooled.

Judy Reibel

Best Ever Brownies

4 squares unsweetened
   chocolate
¼ pound unsalted butter
¼ pound unsalted margarine
1 tablespoon instant expresso
2 cups sugar
3 eggs, well beaten
1 teaspoon vanilla
1 cup flour
¼ teaspoon salt
1 cup chopped pecans

Mint Frosting:
3 tablespoons butter or
   margarine
1½ cups powdered sugar
1¼ teaspoons peppermint
   frosting
1½ tablespoons cream
red food coloring
Topping:
2 squares bakers chocolate,
   melted
2 tablespoons butter

Combine chocolate, margarine and butter, and espresso powder in top of a double boiler over simmering water. Melt, stirring occasionally. Remove from heat. Add sugar, eggs and vanilla. Mix well. Sift together flour and salt and add to chocolate mixture. Stir well and fold in nuts. Pour into greased and floured 9 inch square pan. Bake in 350 degree oven for 45 minutes. When done brownies will be glossy, but inside should be moist.

Mint Frosting: Cream butter and mix powdered sugar. Add enough cream to make smooth and add flavoring and food coloring. Spread on cooled brownies and freeze 15 minutes.

Topping: Drizzle on top 2 squares bakers chocolate melted and mixed with 2 tablespoons butter.

Lucille Hallisey

Fruitcake Brownies

4 squares unsweetened
  chocolate
¹/₂ pound butter or margarine
  (2 sticks)
2 cups sugar
4 eggs
1 teaspoon vanilla extract
1¹/₂ teaspoons rum extract
²/₃ cup all-purpose flour

¹/₂ teaspoon salt
¹/₂ cup walnut pieces, pea size
¹/₂ cup sweetened flaked or
  shredded coconut, firmly
  packed
¹/₂ cup chocolate chips
¹/₂ cup glacé cherries, cut in
  quarters, firmly packed

Melt the chocolate and the butter or margarine slowly together in an open saucepan or in an open container in a microwave oven. Pour the mixture into a mixing bowl and stir in the sugar. Beat in the eggs and vanilla. Stir in the flour and salt just until mixed. Stir in the remaining ingredients with a few brief strokes. Bake in an oiled 9x13 inch pan at 350 degrees for 30 to 40 minutes, or until a toothpick inserted in the center comes out barely clean. Cool completely before cutting into small bars or squares.

Karen Wiskoff

Low-Cal Cheese Cake

1 (10 ounce) can pineapple
  slices
¹/₃ cup pineapple juice
  (drained from can of
  pineapple slices)
15 ounces ricotta cheese

1 envelope unflavored gelatin
1 egg
1¹/₂ teaspoons lemon juice
3 packages sweetener
dash cinnamon

Drain pineapple and dissolve gelatin in ¹/₃ cup juice. Put everything except gelatin mixture in a blender and mix. Add gelatin mixture and blend again. Pour into a Teflon pan, sprinkle with cinnamon and bake at 350 degrees for 50 minutes.

Judy Reibel

Marta's Cheesecake

2 cups flour
1 cup sugar
3 egg yolks
2 tablespoons lemon juice
1 tablespoon rum
1 tablespoon brandy
8 ounces unsalted margarine
   or butter

Cheese Filling:
8 ounces cream cheese
16 ounces low fat cottage
   cheese
4 eggs
1 cup sugar
1 tablespoon rum
1 tablespoon brandy
1 teaspoon baking powder

Cut margarine into the flour. Stir in the egg yolks and the rest of the cheesecake ingredients and knead the dough. Let the dough rest in the refrigerator at least overnight. Can be kept in the refrigerator for about 1 week. Divide dough in two and pat the dough evenly into buttered springform pans. It should be ¼ inch thick. Make a roll of the dough, about ¼ inch thick, and press evenly and lightly around the edge of the pans.

Cheese Filling: Separate the egg yolks, keeping the whites in the refrigerator. Put yolks in a blender and add the sugar. Slowly add the cottage cheese, then rum and brandy. Mix until fluffy and almost liquid. Cut the cream cheese into about 5 pieces and add them one at a time. Then add the baking powder. Beat the egg whites in a large bowl until stiff. Fold this into the cream cheese mixture and pour into the prepared dough. Bake for 1½ hours at 325 degrees.

Yields 2 cakes of about 9¹/₂ inches.

Marta Weltsch

Cheesecake

Crust:
2 cups quick cooking oats
³/₄ cup finely chopped nuts
³/₄ cup firmly packed brown
  sugar
¹/₂ cup melted butter

Filling:
4 (8 ounce) packages cream
  cheese
3 (1 pint) cartons sour cream
2 cups sugar
6 eggs
2 teaspoons vanilla
juice of 1 large lemon
¹/₂ teaspoon cinnamon

Combine all ingredients for the crust. Firmly press into bottom and sides of 11 inch springform pan. Bake at 350 degrees for 18 minutes or until brown.

Filling: Mix all ingredients except ¹/₂ pint of sour cream and cinnamon. Beat with electric mixer until very smooth. Pour into crust and bake at 325 degrees for 75 to 90 minutes. Cool 5 minutes. Mix sour cream with cinnamon. Spread over cake and bake again at 350 degrees for 15 minutes.

Serves 12.

Betsy Rosenthal

Cathleen's Cheesecake

Crust:
2¹/₂ cups graham cracker
  crumbs
¹/₂ to ³/₄ cube butter or
  margarine, melted
Filling:
4 whole eggs
1 (16 ounce) package cream
  cheese
1 pint sour cream

1 teaspoon vanilla
juice of 1 lemon
rind of 1 lemon
¹/₂ cup flour
1 cup sugar
Topping:
1 pint sour cream
¹/₄ cup sugar
¹/₂ teaspoon vanilla

Mix crust and put in bottom of 10 inch springform pan. Bake for 8 to 10 minutes in a 400 degree oven. Mix all filling ingredients until smooth and creamy and pour into the pan. Bake at 350 degrees for 1 hour. During last 10 minutes of baking, spread topping mixture on and continue baking. Remove from oven and cool. Refrigerate overnight.

Cathleen Connell

Cheesecake without Guilt

Wafer Crust:
4 graham crackers, ginger
   snaps or other cookies,
   crushed
Filling:
1 carton 1 percent low-fat
   cottage cheese
16 ounces low fat cream cheese

1¼ cups sugar, divided
2 eggs
1 teaspoon vanilla
3 tablespoons unsweetened
   chocolate (optional)
4 egg whites
¼ teaspoon cream of tartar

Place crushed graham crackers or cookies in bottom of springform pan. Mix cottage cheese and cream cheese in food processor or blender, until smooth. Add 1 cup sugar, 2 eggs and vanilla. Mix until smooth. Take 3 cups of this mixture and set aside.

To remaining mixture in bowl, add chocolate and 2 tablespoons sugar. Process until smooth. Set aside.

Beat egg whites and cream of tartar at high speed. Add remaining 2 tablespoons sugar to that, 1 tablespoon at a time, until stiff peaks form. Fold ³/₄ of it into vanilla mixture. Fold ¼ of it into chocolate mixture. Spoon into pan. Swirl with knife at once, to mix. Bake at 325 degrees for 50 minutes. Cool 15 minutes at room temperature. Cover and chill at least 8 hours before serving. Only 203 calories per slice.

Cathleen Connell and Diana Rosenthal

Creamy Cheese Cake

12 ounces cream cheese	graham crust
2 eggs, beaten	Topping:
3/4 cup sugar	1 cup sour cream
2 teaspoons vanilla	3 1/2 tablespoons sugar
1/2 teaspoon lemon juice	1 teaspoon vanilla

Combine cheese cake ingredients. Beat until light and frothy. Pour into graham crust and bake at 350 degrees for 15 to 20 minutes. Remove and cool for 5 minutes, then pour topping over pie and bake 10 minutes more.

Jinx Havas and Grandma Havas

Chocolate Cheesecake

1/4 cup water	3 (8 ounce) packages cream
1 1/3 cups semi-sweet chocolate	cheese, at room
chips	temperature
1 cup crushed chocolate	1 cup sugar
wafers (about 20)	2 eggs
1/4 cup margarine or butter,	1 cup sour cream
melted	1 teaspoon vanilla

Combine wafer crumbs and butter. Press mixture into the bottom of a 9 inch springform pan and set aside. In a small saucepan, heat the water to boil. Reducing heat to low add chocolate pieces and stir until melted. In a large bowl, cream cheese until light and fluffy. Add sugar and eggs and continue beating until well blended. Add melted chocolate and beat at low speed. Add sour cream and vanilla and continue beating until well blended. Pour batter into prepared pan. Bake at 350 degrees for 55 to 60 minutes. The sides will be puffed and the center soft. The cake will firm as it cools. Place cake on wire rack and cool for several hours before removing the sides of the pan. Garnish with powdered sugar and chocolate curls. Serve at room temperature. To freeze: wrap well and freeze up to four months. Thaw at room temperature for 3 to 4 hours before serving.

Phyllis Torin

An Old Family Apple Pie and Pie Crust

Pie Crust: (Makes 2)
2 cups flour
1 cup shortening
1/2 cup water, milk or juice
1 dash salt
Apple Pie Filling:
5 to 7 cups apples, cored and
    peeled

3/4 cup sugar, or less
1 teaspoon lemon juice
1/2 teaspoon cinnamon
1/4 teaspoon nutmeg
1 pinch salt
2 tablespoons butter

This is a recipe I learned from my mother that she learned from her mother. It is simple to remember because the portions always decrease by one half. The secret is to work fast, don't over-handle the dough and use cold liquid. Refrigerating dough before rolling out seems to increase the flakiness.

Put flour in mixing bowl, cut in shortening quickly to size of small peas. Moisten mixture with liquid till it just holds together. (You may not need entire amount of liquid). Form into ball with hands and proceed as above. Be sure to flour rolling pin and dough lightly to prevent sticking; you may use stockinette cover. Crust may also be rolled out between two sheets of wax paper, lightly floured. Cut dough into two parts, one slightly larger than the other, place on a lightly floured board and pat quickly into a thick, flat disk. Roll lightly from the center out, in all directions (about 1/8 inch thick). Lift pastry into pan without stretching. For a well baked bottom crust, pre-bake shell in hot oven for 5 minutes.

Mix thinly sliced apples with all ingredients except butter. Put in pastry-lined pan, heaping high in center, dot with butter. Moisten edge of bottom crust, cover with top crust, flute or press with tines of fork. Make several slits in top crust. Bake in 450 degree oven for 15 minutes. Reduce heat to 350 degrees and bake 35 minutes or until crust is brown or until juice bubbles through slits on top of pie.

Maureen Chodosh

Mom's Apple Pie

1 (10 inch) unbaked pie crust
4 large Pippin apples
1/2 cup sugar
2 tablespoons flour
2 tablespoons lemon juice

1 tablespoon lemon zest
nutmeg
1 cube butter
1/2 cup flour
1/4 cup sugar

Mix sliced apples, sugar, flour, lemon juice and zest and nutmeg and place in unbaked pie shell. Mix butter, second flour and sugar and crumble over apple mix. Bake 1 hour at 425 degrees.
Serves 6 to 8.

Joyce Kurtz

Caramel Topped Apple Pie

5 1/2 cups apples, sliced
1/4 cup water
1 (9 inch) pastry shell
3/4 cup sugar
3/4 cup graham cracker
    crumbs
1 tablespoon flour

1/4 teaspoon salt
1/2 teaspoon cinnamon
1/2 teaspoon nutmeg
1/2 cup pecans, chopped
1/3 cup butter, melted
1/2 pound caramel candies
1/2 cup milk, hot

Put sliced apples and water in saucepan; cover and steam 3 minutes. Turn out on cookie sheet to cool quickly; arrange in unbaked pie pastry. Combine remaining ingredients, except caramels and hot milk, and sprinkle over apples. Bake in 425 degree oven for 10 minutes; reduce heat to 350 degrees and bake 20 minutes. While pie is baking, melt the caramels and milk together in double boiler. Pour the hot caramel sauce over the top of the pie and continue baking for 10 minutes more. Cool before serving.

Mimi Weingarten

Derby Pie

1 cup sugar
1/2 cup flour
2 eggs, beaten
1/4 pound margarine, melted
  and cooled

1 cup pecans, broken
1 (6 ounce) package semi-
  sweet chocolate bits
1 teaspoon vanilla
2 tablespoons bourbon

Mix sugar and flour. Add eggs, margarine, pecans, unmelted chocolate and vanilla. Pour in unbaked pie shell. Bake at 325 degrees for 1 hour. Serve warm with whipped cream.

For deep dish pie shell, make 1 1/2 times recipe, but keep amount of chocolate chips and pecans the same.

Serves 8.

Susan Greenbaum

Ricotta Berry Pie

1 (9 inch) pastry shell
2 1/2 cups fresh blackberries,
  or unsweetened frozen
3/4 cup sugar
1 1/2 tablespoons quick cooking
  tapioca
1/2 teaspoon cinnamon

8 ounces ricotta cheese
1 egg, separated
1/4 teaspoon salt
1/2 cup half and half cream
1 tablespoon lemon juice
3/4 teaspoon lemon rind,
  grated

Line a 9 inch pan with pastry. Mix together the berries (you may use any blackberry type such as olallieberries), 1/2 cup of the sugar, the tapioca and cinnamon until blended. Let stand 5 minutes. In blender container, combine the ricotta, egg yolk, salt, half and half, remaining 1/4 cup sugar, lemon juice, and peel; blend until smoothly pureed. Beat egg white until soft peaks form; fold in cheese mixture just until blended. Spoon the berry mixture into the pastry; evenly spread over cheese mixture. Bake in a 425 degree oven for 10 minutes; reduce heat to 350 degrees and continue baking 30 minutes or until topping appears firm when dish is gently shaken.

Joyce Kurtz

French Lemon Pie

1 (10 inch) unbaked pie shell
1 teaspoon flour
1 tablespoon cornmeal
1½ cups sugar
4 eggs
½ cup milk
¼ cup lemon juice
4 tablespoons lemon zest
½ cup butter or margarine, melted

Beat eggs until very light, add sugar and beat well. Add flour, cornmeal, lemon juice, zest and milk. Add melted butter or margarine last.

Pour into unbaked pie shell and bake for 10 minutes at 350 degrees. Lower oven to 275 degrees and continue to bake for 45 minutes. Forms a brown crust on top.

Serves 8.

Joyce Kurtz

Gourmandise Dessert Cheese Ball

8¾ ounces canned crushed pineapple in juice
8 ounces Gourmandise cheese, softened
6 ounces cream cheese, softened
½ cup pecans, chopped

Drain pineapple, reserving 2 tablespoons juice. Beat 2 cheeses and 2 tablespoons juice until well blended. Stir in pineapple. Shape into ball. Roll in nuts. Chill until served. Serve with crackers and assorted fruits. (We use pears and apples.)

Gail and Dennis Bates

Pizza Pan Peanut Brittle

1 cocktail peanuts, large jar   2 tablespoons water
1/2 pound butter   1 teaspoon vanilla
1 cup sugar

Spread nuts on pizza pan. In heavy saucepan, melt butter. Add sugar and water. Cook, stirring constantly until mixture turns caramel color (hard crack). Add vanilla and mix quickly. Spread over peanuts while very hot. Cool and place in freezer or refrigerator several hours. Break apart. (For a change of pace, try cashews instead of peanuts.)

Linda Kaiser

Non-Fat Raspberries Gratin

1 pint (2 cups) raspberries or   5 tablespoons dark brown
    blackberries   sugar
1 cup non-fat sour cream

Preheat broiler. Place 1/2 cup berries in each of 4 (4 inch) soufflé or gratin dishes. Stir sour cream. Spread 1/4 cup over each dish of berries, spreading almost, but not to the edge of the dish. Push 1 1/4 tablespoons brown sugar through a strainer over each dish, mounding slightly in the middle. Place 3 to 4 inches under broiler. Broil until sugar just begins to caramelize and bubble.

Serves 4.

Mocha Soufflé

6 tablespoons butter, room temperature	1 cup milk, scalded
12 tablespoons sugar	3 tablespoons flour
3 squares chocolate	³/₄ teaspoon vanilla
3 tablespoons coffee liqueur	3 egg yolks
	6 egg whites

You will need 6 small individual soufflé dishes (use ¹/₃ of total measured butter and ¹/₃ total sugar and coat dishes).

Heat chocolate, coffee liqueur, remaining sugar, scalded milk in double boiler over simmering water. Melt remaining butter in pan and equal amount of flour. Stir until smooth. Gradually add chocolate mixture. Add egg yolks, vanilla and remove from heat. Beat egg whites until stiff. Carefully fold into chocolate mixture. Divide into 6 dishes and bake in preheated 375 degree oven 15 to 20 minutes until puffy, springy and bouncy.

Charles Beren

Swedish Rice Pudding

2 cups milk	¹/₄ teaspoon cinnamon
2 eggs, slightly beaten	¹/₂ cup quick cooking rice
¹/₂ cup sugar	¹/₂ cup raisins
1 teaspoon vanilla	

Measure milk in 4 cup glass measure. Microwave on high for 5 to 5¹/₂ minutes or until hot. Combine eggs, sugar, vanilla and cinnamon in 1¹/₂ quart glass casserole; mix well. Stir in rice, raisins and hot milk. Cover with glass lid or plastic wrap. Microwave on defrost for 12 to 13 minutes or until set. Let stand covered for 5 minutes before serving.

Note: Cover is used on rice pudding so rice stays soft and light.

Serves 6.

Ann Packer

Blueberry Bread Pudding

12 slices homemade-type white bread	1 cup blueberries
16 ounces non-fat cream cheese	3 cups egg substitute
	1/3 cup maple syrup
	2 cups non-fat milk

Remove crusts from bread and cut into 1 inch cubes. Place half of bread cubes in 9x13 inch baking dish sprayed with non-stick spray. Cut cheese into 1 inch cubes and scatter over bread cubes. Scatter blueberries over cheese. Place other half of bread over blueberries. Mix milk, "eggs" and syrup together and pour over bread. Cover with foil and place in refrigerator overnight. Bake covered, in preheated 350 degree oven for 30 minutes. Uncover and bake 30 minutes more. Will be puffy and golden when done.

Serves 6 for brunch.

Beth Weissman

Persimmon Pudding

1 cup very ripe persimmon pulp	2 teaspoons baking soda
1 cup sugar	1 cup flour
1/2 cup milk	1/2 cup walnuts, chopped
1/2 teaspoon salt	Hard Sauce:
1/2 teaspoon vanilla	1/2 cube butter
1/4 teaspoon cinnamon	1 cup powdered sugar
1 tablespoon melted butter	brandy

Starting with the persimmon pulp, add each succeeding ingredient and beat until well blended. Pour into a greased loaf pan and bake 45 minutes in a 350 degree oven.

Hard Sauce: This rich winter dessert is best served with hard sauce made by mixing 1/2 cube butter with about 1 cup powdered sugar and enough brandy to thin to a thick frosting consistency.

Joyce Kurtz

Cranberry Dessert

1 cup canned whole berry cranberry sauce or strained	2 to 3 large ripe bananas

Quantity can be varied to taste or what you have on hand. Put ingredients in food processor for a short time on the pulse cycle until blended together. Spoon in dessert glasses and chill in the refrigerator until ready to serve.

Barbara Lewit

Rhubarb and Strawberry Dessert

1 pint fresh strawberries 5 stalks fresh rhubarb	1 package strawberry gelatin

Wash and stem berries; cut rhubarb into cubes; place berries and rhubarb into pot with enough water to cover the fruit. Bring to a boil and remove from heat. Add the strawberry gelatin and stir until fully dissolved. Pour into dessert cups and chill.

Anna Shelkowsky

English Toffee Bars

1 cup butter or margarine
1 cup brown sugar
1 egg yolk
1 teaspoon vanilla

1½ cups flour
1½ German sweet chocolate
   bars
¼ cup pecans

Cream butter and sugar; add yolk and vanilla and continue to cream. Gradually add flour. Spread on lightly greased rimmed cookie sheet and bake for 15 to 18 minutes in a 375 degree oven. Melt the chocolate in a double boiler. Pour chocolate over cookie as soon as it's removed from the oven. Sprinkle with nuts. Immediately cut in diamond shapes and cool in the pan.

E-Z Microwave Dessert

2 regular boxes chocolate
   pudding
4 cups milk

1 (14 ounce) box cinnamon
   flavored graham crackers
1 small container non-dairy
   whipped topping

Mix pudding and milk together and cook on high in microwave for 10 minutes, stirring once during cooking. Place ⅓ of the graham crackers in the bottom of a 9x13 inch pan; then cover with ⅓ of the pudding mix; continue layering. Finish with a layer of non-dairy topping and serve.

JoAnne Rockower

Complete with a mock wedding, strolling traditional Eastern European klezmer musicians, and costumed villagers, our Jewish Food Festival in Carmel has evolved over the last seven years into an event recreating the richness of life in a mythical Eastern European Jewish village, or shtetl. We based our shtetl on Shalom Alecheim's Anatevka, the home of the various "Fiddler on the Roof" characters. In reality, life was bitterly hard, but as the distance of time and space increases, reality fades and fanciful memories of bitter and bittersweet take their place. Our Jewish Food Festival offers all the edible delights available on the Sabbath and holidays. Only the rich in any shtetl could have afforded to consume them on any other day. The more contemporary California-Jewish versions are on the menu as well. Storytellers, videos on shtetl life, Israeli dancing, arts and crafts, art exhibitions and other educational experiences all unite the Jew and non-Jew to take part in the shared experience of an ancestral home from where any of us might have originated. The photos included were all taken at the Food Festival.

Index

Congregational Beth Israel
5716 Carmel Valley Road
Carmel, California 93923

Please send _____ copy(ies)   @ $13.95 each _____
     Postage and handling   @ $3.00 each _____
     California residents add sales tax   @ $1.01 each _____
                                            Total _____

Name _____

Address _____

City _____ State_____ Zip _____

Make checks payable to *Congregation Beth Israel.*

Congregational Beth Israel
5716 Carmel Valley Road
Carmel, California 93923

Please send _____ copy(ies)   @ $13.95 each _____
     Postage and handling   @ $3.00 each _____
     California residents add sales tax   @ $1.01 each _____
                                            Total _____

Name _____

Address _____

City _____ State_____ Zip _____

Make checks payable to *Congregation Beth Israel.*

Congregational Beth Israel
5716 Carmel Valley Road
Carmel, California 93923

Please send _____ copy(ies)   @ $13.95 each _____
     Postage and handling   @ $3.00 each _____
     California residents add sales tax   @ $1.01 each _____
                                            Total _____

Name _____

Address _____

City _____ State_____ Zip _____

Make checks payable to *Congregation Beth Israel.*